FACING YOUR FEARS

How to Deal with Your Bully and Win the Day

Carlito N. Somera
Award-Winning Author

10-10-10
Publishing

#FACING YOUR FEARS: How to Deal with Your Bully and Win the Day

ISBN: 978-1-77277-414-6

Published by:
10-10-10 Publishing
Markham, Ontario

Contents

To the Dene Tha' First Nation children and youth
for allowing me to serve and grow with you.
I learned so much about my precious
life experiences by spending time with you
in your community,
which I call home.

To my children: Jessica, James, and Joshua,
my source of inspiration,

I dedicated this book to all of you.

FOREWORD

I first met Carlito N. Somera at one of my workshops, and I noticed that he was engaged and attentively deciphering and digesting everything I said. I am very excited about Carlito's intention to support his community through the writing of this book.

Facing Your Fears is about a courageous First Nations boy who would like to create social change by eliminating bullies in the school and extend that growth outside of his community.

I spent considerable time reading this book, and I strongly encourage you to get your copy! This book recognizes the power of believing in the teachings that your parents and grandparents shared with you as you grew up. No matter what challenges you encounter, no matter how tough your life might be, the power within you will help you to come out strong.

Facing Your Fears will guide your healing journey internally and lead you to a new life perspective.

Raymond Aaron
New York Times Bestselling Author

ACKNOWLEDGMENTS

My ardent desire to publish my book rekindled when I had the time to reflect on my life journey during the pandemic. The honour is mine as I have been a part of the Dene Tha' First Nation Community for more than a decade and have been inspired by my life experience.

I am so proud of my daughter, Jessica, who shared my passion for accomplishing my book. She said, *"Dad, I had a dream that you finished your book, and you were signing them at your book launch!"* From that time on, I kept writing my book because I didn't want to fail her dream.

I appreciate my two sons, James and Joshua, who are very independent and give me my time to write. They played basketball without me. I also thanked my wife, Dina, who gave me space to work on my project.

I am grateful to Ms. Lori Aliche, my best mentor, to guide me by grounding myself and becoming a better leader. We have worked together since 2007, and she has been my tandem in trying to effect change in our students' lives.

I am also grateful and indebted to Mrs. Virginia Alarcon and Roberto Alarcon, who acted as my parents here in Canada. Thank you for being there for me, especially when I needed you the most.

I want to thank my colleague, Ronan (RJ) MacDonald, who worked 24/7 in guiding young people. His support, wisdom, and experience are instrumental for me to grow as a school administrator.

I want to thank my friends, Yhong M. and Randy S., for their support to me to become a strong educational leader.

I am also grateful to Dr. Jane Simington, my facilitator, for courses that covered trauma recovery, suicide prevention, grief, and loss. The knowledge and skills that I learned from these courses guided me to become a better teacher, counselor, and leader.

I am indebted and grateful for life, to the Dene Tha' Chief and Council and its members, for allowing me to serve the nation for more than a decade. I have fulfilled my dream, which bloomed where I started. The DTFN is the first community that trusted my skills, being a foreign-trained teacher. I learned to adopt the reserve as my home. I learned about the culture and loved the community, people, and children.

I am also grateful to the DTFN Health and Community and Wellness for our Sports and Health Program support. Your help in ensuring our children's health means so much to me, and I can be sure that our children are healthy and ready for learning every day.

Acknowledgments

I sincerely appreciated Jacinth Brissett for connecting me with Raymond Aaron and his team. Ms. Brissett inspired me so much because I saw her end product. She has a positive attitude that just magnetizes people to keep moving forward and achieve their dreams.

Raymond Aaron, a bestselling author, has inspired and motivated me to gain tons of knowledge from his expertise. He also opens up another door of opportunity to help the community that I am committed to serving. I am indebted to you for enhancing my skills and providing me another milestone for my life journey. This 10-10-10 workshop has turned my dream into reality.

I am also so grateful to Chinmai Shammy for sharing business strategies and experiences that serve as my guide to fulfilling my dream as an author. Your invaluable advice has made my book more appealing to my audience.

I am also grateful to Grace Alarcon Isla and her family, my friend, and my adoptive sister. They also shared her passion for education and considered my family as part of hers.

I am also grateful to Sally Manghi, Andy, and Camillo, the family of Dr. Norma P. Olaya, for considering me as their relative. Dr. Norma P. Olaya had a significant impact on my educational achievement. God blessed her spirit and soul.

I would also like to thank Walter Beaulieu, the Big Bear, for letting me use his masterpiece at the back of this book. Walter is a handyman, and he always saved the day when I needed his help.

I would also like to thank our Class of 1990, MCC BS Education Alumni, Kuya Jojo, along with Ate Elda, Kuya Rey, Lyn, Josephine, and Emma, my closest friends from afar, for cheering me on. Thank you, Kuya Jojo, for promoting my book through DZJO Spirit FM 101.7 and DWBW 92.1 FM Radyo TV Baler.

I would also like to thank Kuya Resty, my first friend and mentor during my first year of teaching at Mt. Carmel High School, San Luis. Thank you for keeping in touch.

I would also like to recognize the spiritual support of Fr. Ben and Sister Rose. Thank you for your prayers and for keeping me with my Catholic faith.

I would like to thank Mr. Enrique Parrocha, my former principal and mentor from the Philippines, who always kept in contact with me, keeping up with my career and family. His wisdom has served as my inspiration on my life journey in a foreign land.

I would also like to acknowledge Oprah Winfrey for her YouTube videos, which are among the sources of my inspirations: "The Secret of My Success" and "You Become What You Believe!" I learned a lot from these videos. Oprah set her life from a very young age, and she thought that she could live a life better than what she observed in the family. She worked hard to achieve the future she envisioned.

I would also like to acknowledge Steve Harvey for his YouTube videos: "Steve Harvey's Success Journey" and "The Steve Harvey Motivational Speech That Made Obama Cry 2020." His life story is very inspirational. Lessons from his father, the hardships and failures he experienced, and his dream to be on TV resonated so much with me. You need to write your goal down, and that would be your vision in life.

I would also like to acknowledge my colleagues—Hayley, Rhoda, Dakota P., Judyann, Beatriz, and Roleine—and the rest of the DTCS staff for such fantastic support in the workplace. During summer vacation and being one phone call away, your presence has pushed me to keep on my story.

I would also like to acknowledge Brian and Matt from Ever Active Schools for supporting our programs. Thank you for your generosity and trust that involved our Indigenous youth in becoming mentors.

Through the Communities Choosewell program, I would like to acknowledge the Alberta Recreation and Physical Activity Division for providing us grants to continue our Grow Tower program. Thank you, Marissa and Janet, for all your follow-up and support.

I would also like to acknowledge Ashraf Abou Moustafa, the Flamingo Inn owner, who opens up his hotel for our staff. Ashraf is a very generous and kind person who goes out of his way to help people.

I would also like to acknowledge Tolko Industries Ltd for supporting our school programs—breakfast program and tree planting program—and for their dedication to building relationships with our school.

I would also like to thank Mark and Suzie, owners of the Canadian Tire, High Level, who donated a considerable amount of sports equipment to the school to promote active and healthy living for the children and the community. Thank you for your constant support to encourage children to play team-structured sports, a proactive approach to eradicating bullying.

I would also like to thank Tess, the Dollar Store owner, High Level, for allowing us to get some supplies from her store through purchase orders. I am thankful for your trust and generosity.

To the CFWE, CKYL, and KIX FM radio stations, our sister radio stations for our CKCS/CKCA provided us the opportunity to air our information to our local community coverage area. Having a radio station in the school will help our children enhance their communication skills and succeed academically.

I would also like to thank Global News, Edmonton, for providing us fresh and daily news. I watch your program every day.

A special thank you to Jordan Maskell of Echo Newspaper for writing the articles that I shared. You are very instrumental in informing our readers about the school's happenings.

I want to thank North Peace Tribal Council for providing help to the Four Nations in the Mackenzie Region. Thank you for helping families and children in our community.

I would also like to thank N'deh Corporation for donating backpacks to our children. Thank you for your generosity and continuous support in the education of our children.

Acknowledgments

I would also like to thank Kevin Independent Store for allowing us to get products through purchase orders. Thank you for your trust in doing business with us.

I would also like to thank Mr. Michael MacMann, superintendent of Fort Vermilion School Division, for allowing me to attend the principal's meeting to learn some leadership skills. Thank you for extending your services to work with your academic supervisors.

I am grateful to Alberta Education for awarding my permanent teacher's license and enabling me to have a Leadership Qualifications Service Certificate.

I am grateful to all my friends out there who remain incognito. Your continuous support is invaluable to the success of this project.

I am very grateful to Andrew Brooke, my editor, who helped me with valuable suggestions and input with my book.

To all of you, my sincerest gratitude. With your support, my story becomes a reality.

CHAPTER 1

The Wailing Locker

Monday morning presents the unknown conditions of children at the Dahmedeh (dah-mi-deh) Community School. Children might have had a difficult weekend due to the lack of amenities in the community. Aside from the non-standard school park and small convenient store, people don't have many choices but to stay home, drink, party, do sewing, paint, beading, and make birch bark baskets. There are not many things to do in the community in terms of having excellent facilities. Those who have vehicles can go to Beram Lake to fish, hunt, and pick wild berries. Seldom, the children would be lucky enough to stay home and play their games. At night, children might not sleep sufficiently due to noise made by people partying or because the house was hosting house bingo until dawn.

"Go to sleep! The medicine man will pull your feet," Marlene told Samuel.

Parents were scaring their children with stories about the notorious medicine man in the community. Children thought the medicine man was the Sasquatch owner, a big, wild, hairy beast in the woods. There were different opinions about the medicine man: There was a good medicine man, and there was one who harmed people somehow. Children were scared, and they would go to bed even on a noisy night. Others would pretend to sleep, but they would still be playing a game installed on their phones or tablets under their covers. Teenagers slept late; they always tended to play online games or be on social media the whole night. Social media has a lot of influence on children's behaviour these days.

There is an emerging pattern of student behaviour every Monday. Sometimes it will extend throughout the whole week. The usual practice is that children seem to be unfocused during child tax day, social assistance day, and payday.

"It must have been hard for you, Samuel, to join the group at the moment. Tell me what happened."

I asked Samuel because he refused to be in the morning circle. As a teacher, one needs to be sensitive to the para-verbals that children are inhibiting.

"Twyla woke me up so early to come to school." He referred to his foster mom.

Twyla's household is quite structured and has expectations. She has children of her own—five of them—and the youngest one is a 10-year-old boy. Twyla can afford to watch at least three foster children in her home. She struggled to wake Samuel up every morning because he slept late, as most kids do. Sometimes, Samuel doesn't have the motivation to go to school due to bullying, so he would pretend to go to school but stay at the back of their house.

"It must have been hard for you to wake up that early. Tell me what you did before going to bed. Let me guess. You played your video games."

I smiled; it was like playing a guessing game. Samuel began to laugh.

"What do you think you could have done to have enough sleep?"

"You're right; you need to go to bed early so that you will have eight hours or more sleep.

The school staff is aware of this trend, so they put different interventions to counteract these chronic issues. The breakfast program helped a lot. Mr. Abedayo was very dedicated to being a one-person army, serving cereal and milk to the children. It has always been cereal and milk, but the children do not complain. It is better to have something in the morning than nothing. By 10:30, students from the different classes will go to Mr. Charles' office to ask for snacks. Even snacks are given free to the children. Behaviour issues are less likely to occur when children are not hungry. Sometimes Mr. Charles will not give them snacks due to lunch being less than an hour away. Children would then not eat their lunch; then afterward, they would be hungry again. Parents should also look after this simple kind of thing, but they put all the onus on the school. When it is something they don't like, they will make a big deal about it, and they will even involve their council.

Strong classroom management skills play a crucial role in the classroom. Students try to push their teacher's buttons, and they like to see how the teacher reacts. Most students are not ready to engage, even though they are already giving work to other students prepared to work.

"Who threw this paper?" Mr. Brandon investigated.

Samuel is crying. He got hit by the crumpled paper.

"You wimp! Skinny faggot frail foster kid!" the note stated.

As usual, the children would not want tattletale on who threw the crumpled paper at Samuel. Everyone laughed and teased Samuel. Samuel's life is so challenging. He was always the subject of ridicule and mocking inside the classroom. Both boys and girls in the class are hard to control. They bully and gang up on weaker students. They always humiliated Samuel because he was a quiet and skinny boy. They made fun of him, and it seemed that they never gave him a rest. Most of the time, he misses class, or he is by himself. He diagnosed Fetal Alcohol Spectrum Disorder (FASD), which was familiar to most children in reserve. They said that this is FASD in its third generation, and the damage is affecting their learning. The diagnosis is not a hindrance for Samuel to live a healthy life. He is a normal, kind, quiet boy who would want other children to treat him as usual.

The unregulated children continued to ruin the day. Mr. Parson struggled to control them, even when just lining up. Instead, students were scurrying everywhere. The EA was yelling at them at the top of her lungs to line up, but it was difficult for students to focus and follow. It was no surprise because it is Monday morning. Children don't have that freedom at home. If relatives were visiting, they would be in their rooms, and when they made noise, adults would yell at them. Most of the time, when relatives visit, they drink and make too much noise, until dawn, so children in the house could not sleep, or if there were a fight, they would end up scared. Parents also fight, and children are scared to death or even get spanked when they don't listen.

Children may be just too excited to go to the gym and play. That was why they ran; however, they still need to learn how to control themselves and follow the rules. The good thing was, they stopped at the front door because they could not open it. During gym time, children don't have the proper footwear. They go with their socks on. It is for safety reasons. There have been many times that the teachers sent notes home, asking parents and guardians to buy proper shoes for their children, but there has been no luck so far. Parents and guardians who understand safety concerns are the only ones who responded to the request. The school gym floor is not that great either. Due to the lack of funding, the gym floor was not up for renovation, and it was not safe for the children to even be rolling on it for any floor exercise.

One Sunday afternoon, in the open gym activities, Mr. Charles and his son played with his co-teacher and other players. James was crying, kneeling on the floor and holding his left knee.

"What happened?" Mr. Charles said.

Mr. Parson was already with James, tending to his knee. Mr. Charles thought that James had banged up his knees.

"There was a sliver in his knee," Mr. Parson answered while James was still crying.

Mr. Charles understood how painful it was to have a sliver in your skin. He checked how bad it was. He used his long fingernails to pluck out the tiny little speck in James' knee, and he wiped and blew on it a little bit.

"You're fine. That is very far from the stomach," Mr. Charles said.

"You're tough on your son," Mr. Parson said to Mr. Charles.

"Don't worry. I love my son more than you know," Mr. Charles responded.

After crying and being relieved of the sliver, James continued playing.

This incident proved that children need to wear proper footwear when using the gym, but it just ends up getting ignored. Mr. Charles bought playing shoes for the basketball players, but it takes many reminders to make sure the players take care of their shoes.

"Where are your shoes, Gerald? Mr. Charles was testing Gerald at that time. He saw him wearing his basketball shoes outside, and they were muddy.

Mr. Charles reminded teachers all the time to keep the doors locked after use because students loved the gym, and they would skip their classes just to play or hide in the equipment room. One time, they did not lock the gym door, and students were trying to hide in the equipment room. Mr. Charles pretended that he did not see that, but he locked them up to scare the children. He got in trouble, and the administration warned him not to do it again. What if he forgot and left the school? What if there was a fire? What would happen to the children? They would be scared to death, and they could sue the school.

Transitioning to the gymnasium was a little bit of a struggle for any teacher in the school. It is crucial to establish all the rules and expectations from the very beginning of the school year. One week to two weeks must be devoted to ensuring that all the children understand the expectations. If the teacher forgot his or her gym key, children would wait by the door, and one needed to go to the front desk to get access; or if missing, they announced it first, and it took a while before the teacher who used, returned it. Just in a blink of an eye, students were everywhere, in the hallway or hiding in the washroom. This scenario was just an ordinary scene in the foyer of the school. The teacher always ignored it because yelling all the time didn't work anymore. Students were immune from being nagged at home, and they took that behaviour to the school. The teachers knew that they needed to be more caring and sensitive to the world these children lived in.

Upon hearing the noise, I swiftly went out of my office to help the teacher. He was the second teacher of this class since the original teacher quit for another neighbouring town job. Even he came back to teach after a couple of years; everything was new again to him from not being around. He led the Grade 7 class, which was the opposite of his teaching assignment before, in high school, where he excelled. Sometimes I don't want to help the teachers because children know that the teacher cannot handle them once the school administrator comes out. Just to show my support, I went out and made sure the children saw me coming. Then they started to go to their line, and they listened to their teacher and then went to their gym class. They almost missed their 30-minute gym time due to behavioural issues.

I walked down the hallway to check their classrooms. I heard someone wailing inside. I scanned through the glass of the door, but I could not see anybody inside. I was sure that someone was crying, and it was coming from the grade seven classroom. I stopped for a while to confirm that I was hearing someone wailing. It was a boy. Maybe someone got hurt, but I could not see anybody. I listened to the wailing carefully. I was sure that it was coming from the locker. It was a wailing locker. I quietly opened a door and searched for the voice. No one was inside, so I began to open the lockers one after another. Finally, in the last locker, I saw Samuel crumpled inside, crying, and wailing like a puppy. With his skinny body, he fit right into the receptacle. He had a rough weekend and looked as though he had not slept well.

"Manser always does this to me, and all the children were laughing at me. The whole class was laughing at me, huh, huh, huh!" Samuel told me, still in his crunched position.

Usually, I could redirect kids acting up and help them regulate themselves and be resilient.

After waiting for two minutes, I began connecting with him. Children just need enough time to process the information they are receiving, which is part of their learning difficulty. As a member of staff, one needs to be cognizant and be sensitive to their feelings. Children need someone to listen to them and respect how they feel. They are young, and they believe you as an adult.

"Hey, Samuel, come to my office, and I will show you something." I encouraged him to get out of his locker.

Samuel took the time to respond, and he always responded well to me. After a couple of minutes, he began to get out of the locker and showed that he was ready to follow me. I put my hand on his shoulder, and we walked together towards my office.

When a child doesn't trust an adult, they will refuse the touch. Therapeutical touch, especially on the shoulder, will help the child fill his sensory needs.

"Did you sleep well last night?" I asked.

On the weekend, most children and youth in reserve play games the whole night, making them sleepy or irritable in class. He said it was too noisy in the house. Samuel, with his three sisters, was living in a crowded foster home. They were in a foster home because their parents were also alcoholics. There were too many people drinking and making lots of noise, and in the end, there was a fight, and the police's siren sounded like hell. He ended up crawling under his bed and plugging his ears with his pillow. No wonder he began his Monday in the opposite direction, with the addition of teasing from Manser and his little gang.

I had known Samuel since he was in kindergarten. Still, I could not remember any remarkable encounter with him, except when he was in Grade 2. There was an unforgettable incident in the washroom. I was walking down to the gymnasium, and Hannah, the language and culture instructor, told me that there was a cry coming from the boy's washroom.

"Mr. Charles, could you check if there is someone in the washroom? I heard a small voice crying," she said.

I followed at once and went into the washroom.

"Hello, is someone in here?" I inquired.

I did not see anyone outside the cubicles, so I proceeded to check each one.

"Mr. Charles, Hu! Hu! Hu!" Samuel was crying.

I smelled a shitty smell. I should have guessed what happened.

"I shit myself," he embarrassingly said.

"It's okay. It's fine. I experienced shitting myself too. I will clean you up!" I assured him.

I left him for a while and grabbed gloves from the kitchen. I went back with additional toilet paper and a change of pants. I never demonstrated in any way that I did not like the poignant smell.

My confidence came from my experience with changing diapers for my younger siblings and my children. I also cleaned junior high students when I worked as an EA at Cloverdale Junior High School in Edmonton.

It was easier to clean up a boy. I wiped up the loose feces that had flowed down his legs and his crotch and everything. He was looking at me with a forced smile.

"Don't worry, Samuel; your secret is safe with me. You're clean now, and I cannot smell anything," I said.

After Samuel got back from his self-embarrassment, I convinced him to go back to the class. It was a long talk, but he finally started walking around to his classroom.

Accidents like that in the school could happen, so teachers requested, from parents, a change of clothes for each student. Being proactive would help a lot more than panicking when something happens.

Samuel, though, was a good artist. I remember when he was in Grade 6. His EA brought his drawing to my office. It was a lovely drawing, but the theme was about death: A boy had hanged himself from a tree. It was an unusual sketch; that was why I called him into the office and provided him some encouraging advice. The drawing reflected the inner feelings of a sad, depressed individual.

"Samuel, you can do better than this kind of drawing. You are a very talented artist. Please draw me a picture of your happy thoughts," I requested.

Hearing those magic words, Samuel got back to his usual self and started drawing beautiful posters again. He usually painted a view of places with lots of colours and flowers. To maximize Samuel's potential and other children's talents, we held a Display Case Colouring Contest, which he won with a unanimous vote from the students. Samuel had the chance to paint the two display cases with chosen students. He was so proud of what he achieved. From that time on, Samuel always gave me something that he drew. I displayed all his drawings on my wall in the office.

That incident with Samuel seemed like a usual scenario in the classrooms. If students could not regulate themselves, they struggled to focus on the teacher.

"EA will stay by the door," the principal said.

This strategy worked at first, but when the students got used to it, they started not listening, and then they looked for another way to get out of the classroom.

"F… off!" Jordan said. "I don't want to work. It's too hard."

Teachers modified the level of their instructions; however, students struggled to follow—not because the teacher did not know how to teach, but the building of trust was not there yet.

When Jordan was feeling that way, he did not use the door that the EA was guarding; instead, he climbed up and jumped out the window. His classmates thought it was fun, so at least three or more students followed him.

"Come back here!" the teacher shouted in a loud tone of voice.

Sometimes teachers were frustrated, and if, within a week, they could not teach, of course, patience would wane, and the frustration levels would go up.

Parents' involvement is crucial to the success of both teaching and learning. Teachers ensure that they follow the proper procedures. The teacher wrote up the incident and tried to reach out to the parents. It was challenging to suspend students. Our goal is to keep students in the school and make sure that we cater to their needs. Sending a student home is like rewarding them because they would like to stay home. We already struggled to maintain good attendance. Suspension, with school work, never worked either, because they would not do it. The most likely thing to work would be an in-school suspension. To involve parents and guardians, the school employed parents to come to school and do one-on-one work with the students, with the teacher's guidance to ensure that they were doing their job.

CHAPTER 2

The Knock Out

T he winter season brings brunt cold temperatures in the northern hemisphere of the world. Classes sometimes are canceled due to the school bus and other vehicles wont to start. Winter is not always bad. It makes the environment beautiful, like heaven. You can see the beauty of sparkling and crystal white snow on the ground. It is delightful for the eyes to see how neat and clean the environment is.

The Dahmedeh First Nation children are not used to doing outdoor activities during wintertime—not because they don't like it, but because parents don't have the patience to bring their children out. During weekdays, children have the chance to go out with their teachers and supervisors. They are all excited to go out because there are lots of things to do outside. The school has small hills of snow to climb up and down. They have a "crazy carpet" to ride down too. Mr. Charles also requested that the maintenance guys make a snow maze so that children would get excited to go out. It is vital to keep the children busy and have supervision; otherwise, throwing snowballs and pushing each other would create chaos and trouble.

It is so strange that the excitement of winter is slowly diminishing for people. They need to be more active and get used to cold weather. "Back in the days," an elder said, "even if it was winter season, we still camped outside, went rabbit snaring, and did some outdoor games."

"This kind of cold winter was nothing for us during my younger days. We had a dog team, and we hauled what we hunted." An elder took pride in sharing that experience with children. When it is minus thirty-five, as stated in the school policy, children are not allowed to go to school; however, the school is open for the staff. There was also a whole week where it was too cold, so the school was closed. One day, the school was closed to everybody due to the weather not improving. It was minus 45 the whole day.

"What happened?" I asked Frank. He was crying down at the office while everyone was lining up for lunch.

I just instructed him to sit down and wait while I was getting my lunch. Usually, I let children wait for a moment to not dwell on their feeling when they got hurt. It was a strategy I discovered through many years of dealing with children's problems. Children are forgiving and can easily forget. When I got back from the office, I repeated what I had asked Frank.

"I was the warrior enemy. I attacked Boomie, left and right, like this." Frank was very animated when he was narrating what had happened. He was proud of what he did. There was no remorse or clue that the act was bullying.

"What are you thinking right now?" I followed up.

"I'd like to choke a kid right now," he proudly replied.

Frank was internalizing what he was playing in his online games. He demonstrated that he was brainwashed and assumed that the situation was a game. Of course, I asked Frank how he could fix it, and he immediately said, "apologize."

"My dad said that I would rather bully than have others bully me," he explained.

"Do you think that is nice, though?" I asked.

"No. I wouldn't want to hurt my friend." He started crying.

I took him back to his class and requested for Boomie. I explained to Boomie what had happened, and I asked the two boys to make restitution. They shook hands and then hugged. Children are children. They went back to class, smiling, and acted as nothing had happened.

It has always been attractive to the students to have a fishing trip to Beram Lake, an old settlement before the devastating flood incident. It has a lot of memorable stories of the elders. This lake has been part of their lives. Even in the cold winter, they were excited to go ice fishing, with the chance to go sledding on the river bank's steep side. They dressed appropriately to make sure that they would not freeze. Children had "crazy carpets" to use. The school also had some extra ones for those who didn't have any. We drove children to the site, closer to the river, while adults drove with their trucks to prepare the spot for the group's arrival. They were the advanced party and started a fire and set up the grill for a barbeque, with hotdogs, moose meat, potatoes, and smores. For adults, they also had their kettle of tea and coffee. Other staff members were just around the fire with their portable chairs because it was too cold outside, especially when the wind blew.

This fishing trip integrated the Traditional Language and Culture program. The program coordinator always invites councilor Sean to join. He made sure that he had the drill to bore holes so that everyone could fish. He also brought some cut logs for firewood and something to sit on while ice fishing. Other students were happy just going up and down the hill with their crazy carpets. Children were laughing and making lots of noise. Supervisors always reminded the children to slow down and be careful. It was an open space, and the environment was so stimulating. It was all fun, but children sometimes are not cautious and forget the safety precautions. There were even a couple of staff members sledding down. It was a great, fun day.

It might be fun for some, but some children are not as sturdy as others. They were scared and, at the same time, slow when it came to sledding. I was a little scared, too, especially when the sled was at its maximum speed. Accidents would be imminent if children were not cautious when sliding down or with which way they followed to climb back up. There was a good chance that sliders could run them over. As expected, others were bumping into each other and crying at the bottom of the slope. Others were just ignoring the pain and coldness. They were more focused on fun and hot dogs to eat. The hot chocolate was also pleasing to the children and the fire's heat, which temporarily killed the cold.

Children were sliding down and climbing back up—back and forth.

"Look at me, Mr. Charles! Look at me!" children shouted.

Mr. Charles waved his hand and smiled at them. He understood that these children always wanted to please adults, like their parents. They could not express those emotions if parents and guardians were not bringing them to this kind of outdoor activity. After some slides, children intermittently went to the fire area, ate hotdogs, drank some juice, and then went back to the top of the slope.

"Be careful! Be careful! Take turns! Take turns!" Mr. Green warned the children, who just took off and slid without warning or clearing at the bottom of the slope.

Seeing Mr. Green struggling, Samuel stepped up and warned people not to be in the way. From the top, he walked down a little bit on the slope and shouted out:

"GUYS, MAKE SURE THERE IS NO ONE ON THE PATH BEFORE YOU SLIDE!"

BANG! Samuel did not get to finish what he was about to say. Someone slid down from the top, scooped him up, and knocked him down so hard that his whole body banged straight down onto the ground.

"I knocked Samuel out, ha ha ha ha ha hah!"

It was Manser who was shouting at the top of his lungs, rejoicing in his victory of having knocked Samuel out by surprise.

"Good for you, little s**t! You're in my way!" he said, without even feeling sorry.

"Who do you think you are…a hero?" Manser said, without saying sorry.

Everyone went quiet and turned their eyes to the slope.

"What happened? What happened? What happened?" Everyone was asking questions.

"HELP! HELP! HELP!" a supervisor yelled.

Samuel was not moving. I rushed to the scene to check on him. He was still unconscious. The impact of his fall had been hard, and it was enough to shake his brain and make him out. Mr. MacDonough, an expert in giving first aid, came to help.

"Hello, first responder! Hello! Hello!"

Nobody picked it up. Maybe the staff was busy chatting in the kitchen or attending to other patients.

"911! 911! Hello! Hello!"

"I can't contact them. Call failed. No signal!"

"We are in a no-signal location. I need to run and look for an area where the signal is."

"Go to the top of the small hill!" Michael yelled.

The connection was more substantial on the small hill's summit. At first, deep snow and freezing weather presented a challenge; however, it did not stop me from rushing in that direction. It was an act of courage, and the action gave me a glimpse of a deer running away for its life. My feet were so cold, and I did not have snow boots for the harsh winter.

"Hello, first responder!" With my first call, no one was responding. Maybe the staff was on their lunch break, or perhaps they were sleeping during lunchtime.

Brrrrrrring. "Please leave a message," it said.

"Hello, first responder. Pick up! Pick up!" I said in my quivering voice. It was my third call, and I was praying that they would pick up.

It brought me the memory of the late councilor, Mastro. The first responder had not picked up the phone at the right time. Hannah, the councilor's wife, called for help from the middle of the cold winter forest. He had a heart attack while hunting. Hannah was asking for help, but it never arrived on time. It took her several calls before she got to speak with somebody on the other line. It was too late to revive Mastro. He had been gone for at least two hours before the rescue arrived.

I could imagine how Hannah felt at that moment. I was trying to call for help, but there was no immediate help available. I had run for at least three kilometers to find a signal on a deep snowy trail, and then I could not get immediate help.

At last, after several attempts, I managed to speak to the community first responder.

"We are at Remba Lake, by the river, where we usually do the ice fishing. We need an ambulance. Samuel got knocked down to the ground and is unconscious. Please help us. Contact 911 because we have a poor connection. Thank you! Do you understand?"

I was thankful that I contacted the first responder, but I was worried about it being another Mastro tragedy in the making. I hoped not. Parents would not let their children go next time if someone died because of this kind of activity. Parents are always concerned about their children's safety. We are too.

Even though I was exhausted and freezing, I decided to walk back to the group. It was hard to walk, and my head began hurting. It was too cold for me, but I made the sacrifice for students' safety in our care.

It took at least an hour and a half to arrive at the scene. The emergency vehicle could not go any faster due to road conditions. Speeding could also cause an accident, and it could delay the rescue.

When I got back, Samuel was still unconscious. Mr. Mac-Donough had been doing all he could to revive him, but it was futile. He decided to wait for at least 15 minutes to see if he would become conscious, but it took time. Our hope was slowly fading. It was a long waiting game for both Samuel and the rescuer.

The hour of fun had faded abruptly, and adults were starting to worry. Their tears began to appear. Other children were crying. They began to go back to the bus as a safe refuge.

"Is Samuel dead? Is Samuel dead?" They were all shocked and were asking questions.

"Ah! Ah! Ah!" Everyone was sighing. They were not pleased about what had happened.

"Well, suck it up!" Ms. Nina said. "If you don't listen and pay attention, that is what will happen. Safety first."

Now, Manser was in big trouble. That incident was what he lived for—to bully other kids at the right time. He did not care what punishment they would give him.

"It's his fault. He was in my way! Good for him, little s**t!"

Instead of feeling sorry for what he did, Manser was even more defensive, blaming Samuel for what happened. But the truth was, he always bullied Samuel anywhere he pleased. It was either in the classroom, in the washroom, or in the park. The boy did not feel remorse about what he did. I was not sure why he did not have empathy for people. Was it because no one taught him? Or because of his well-being?

The howl of a big gray wolf filled the entire Remba Lake area. It was as though the wolf was lamenting that a young lad was gone—or that the wolf smelled an excellent meal. Who knows? Samuel was still not waking up. People all around were wondering why. The howling of the wolves filled the air.

"Children, go back to the bus. We're going back to the school," commanded Mr. Green. "Besides, there might be a lot of wolves by the river bank. It is not safe, especially when you are not listening."

Dahmedeh people believe that wolves are the land's spirit guides; however, they are also cautious because wolves attack humans, especially in the community. Dogs fight wolves, but their strength is not enough to match their ferocity. Their rabies must have been more poisonous.

"Where are they?" they wondered.

The howls of the wolves seemed so close to them, but for some reason, they could not see them, or maybe the wolves were invisible to the naked eye.

The gray wolf licked Samuel's face to wake him up, but it seemed that he was in a profound sleep. It howled and howled and howled. It was trying to summon Samuel's spirit, but it appeared that he was in the deepest part of the universe.

"Screech! Screech! Screech!" Eagles were flying in the sky, in a repeated circular movement, above where Samuel was lying.

"Look at the sky; the eagles are doing tea dancing!" exclaimed a child. The eagles continued to fly in a circle while making the sound of a rhythm, like a drum dance.

Dahmedeh people are superstitious and very spiritual. They associate with their life whatever message they can perceive from the environment.

"Eagles are sending a message to us. We are not going to worry. Samuel will be fine. His spirit guides, the wolf and the eagle are with him on his travel to the spirit world," Elder Billy said.

While they waited for the ambulance to arrive, the elder requested everybody to surround him in a circle. He began to pray with his drum. The combination of the howls of the wolves, the sound of the eagles, and the sound of the elder's drum created the best symphony that anyone could ever hear.

The word of an elder is so powerful and influential. People believe that the elder is their prophet, who brings good news, like Jesus Christ.

A huge bald eagle was looking down sharply at Samuel, trying to reach the depth of his hearing.

After an hour and a half, the medical emergency vehicle arrived. The first aiders were carefully transferred Samuel inside the ambulance and immediately applied first aid. They cleared Samuel's chest and used the emergency automated defibrillator (EAD). After several shocks, they decided to drive out and continue the process on their way to the hospital. They applied all the techniques they could to revive Samuel, but he refused to come to consciousness. They put the oxygen mask on his face. They did not declare whether he was dead or alive, though.

Everyone was slowly getting onto the bus. The children felt the impact of the incident. They were scared that if something happened to Samuel, they would not have any more sledding trips. Their parents would not sign their permission slips.

"How's Samuel?" Liza finally asked Mr. Charles.

"We need to pray. I'm not sure," responded Mr. Charles.

Liza was worried about her little brother. She just sat at the back of the bus. She was quiet and seemed confused about what had happened. Liza was a fragile young girl too. She was on the list for suicide watch. She had attempted to commit suicide due to depression and boyfriend problems. Four of them were living in a foster home, and there was another problem. She needed support and to be with someone all the time.

An incident like this would be a trigger for a relative. If their violent cousin, Limuel, knew about this incident, they could expect that there would be a retaliation.

The students were driven back to their homes. It ended up being an early dismissal. If they went back to the school, they would not be able to concentrate, and the teachers and support staff would have double burnout due to the incident and watching children who could not regulate themselves at any given moment.

Showing a movie was not an option as a strategy to let the kids settle down. When they go home, some of the kids would tell their parents that they just watched a movie, and it was boring. They could watch a film at home. Computer time is a good one, but children always like to play. Computers are for instructions only. Games should be educational, but sometimes the school admin has caught teachers not using the machine properly. You can't blame teachers either. They use computer free time to motivate children to do their work even though they have 24/7 access to a computer in their houses. They play games all the time. It would always go back to parents and guardians on how they set expectations with their children to go to school and co-operate with teachers to succeed academically. The best way is to think of it as always being a brand new day and starting fresh for tomorrow.

CHAPTER 3

Samuel's Dream

T he light was so bright that it was enough to illuminate the entire universe, but it might just be the sun shining in broad daylight during a cold winter day. Samuel expected to hear the crisp sound of frozen, hard snow, but to his wonder, there was a deafening silence. His feet didn't feel anything hard—just a smooth, flowing, fluffy, thick cloud. He kept walking, going towards the source of the light. Samuel thought it was the never-ending Remba River, but he was wrong. It seemed that the beam was leading to the peak of the universe. He felt as though, with every step he took, that he was ascending to the sky.

"Am I dreaming? Where am I?" Samuel wondered.

"Hoooooooooowl!"

"Hoooooooooowl!"

"Screeeeeeeh!"

"Screeeeeech!"

The gray wolf and the bald eagle were simultaneously making their sounds to wake Samuel up. He slowly stretched his body, moved his hands, and tried to squeeze his eyes. He sat down, looked around, and then saw the big gray wolf and the bald eagle up in the sky. The scene projected energy towards Samuel, and he felt strong as he noticed the changes in his body. Any little noise around seemed to become louder. He could see a tiny object far away, and it was as though it were close to him. The gray wolf started to run at high speed, and, all of a sudden, Samuel found himself running with it at a tremendous and extraordinary speed. The bald eagle kept making a high-pitched noise while following the two speedrunners. Samuel could not believe that he could run as fast as the wolf. After running for quite a distance, they ended up in a small, old cabin in the wood. The door automatically opened. The bald eagle swooped down to the open door while the gray wolf entered humbly. Samuel followed the two animals without any hesitation. Inside the cabin, an older man was smiling at Samuel.

"Welcome, Samuel, my little Chief Teen. I am your Grandpa, Jimmy," the old man said.

"I always dreamt of you, Grandpa. You always visited me in my dreams," Samuel responded.

The grandpa said that he had always watched Samuel's life: how he grew up and how good he was as a growing lad.

"Samuel, our culture is dying. Fewer and fewer people are practicing our culture. What will happen to the younger generation if all the elders are gone? I see these young people; some don't have any respect for our culture anymore. Seldom do they go hunting or trapping; they are leaving all our old ways. They drink and fight. They commit murder. They do drugs, and they just let their young ones raise themselves. Young people are dying due to alcohol. You need to go back there and restore our culture and maintain peace in our land," Grandpa Jimmy said.

"Grandpa, I'm scared. Manser bullies me all the time. My classmates always laugh at me," Samuel exclaimed.

"Not this time, because you are the Chief Teen, the hero of our land," Grandpa Jimmy explained.

"How can I do that, Grandpa? I am small and weak," Samuel reasoned.

"Samuel, my grandson, we live by sharing our traditional teachings to our young people, and that starts from home. If those young bullies received those teachings at home, there would not be any bullies anywhere. The family is the foundation of values and discipline. Growing up, Grandpa Jimmy would be holding a moose-hide scroll, and our parents made sure that we knew our teachings. When we had some meat, we needed to share it with everybody. We helped one another as a community. We cared for one another as brothers and sisters. We looked after each other as one big family. Respect was paramount. We respected our elders and everything around us—nature, the animals. We only hunted what we needed, and we thanked the Creator for looking after us. We had complete rest, so we slept at night and worked when it was light out. When someone shared some ideas, we did not argue, and we made sure that we were all polite. Young people, both boys, and girls should behave respectfully and adequately.

"Did you notice anything while you were running?" Grandpa Jimmy asked.

"No," Samuel said.

"Samuel, did you not see the wolf and the eagle? They are your bits of help. Were you not running with my wolf? Did you feel tired?" Grandpa Jimmy explained again. Samuel felt that it was just a reasonable speed and strength that he had exerted, but it was extraordinary strength and speed.

"Bullying stops here," Grandpa Jimmy continued. "You need to take action before it creates a negative impact on you and other people. Ignoring is not the right solution for harmful and mean people. You need to take a stand. You need to push back and show him that you are not scared anymore. You need to point out and tell that bully that it is not our culture to bully our kind. Prepare yourself for the encounter, but don't attack him. Let him come to you and take control of yourself."

"Do you know someone in your school that you can trust?" Grandpa Jimmy inquired.

"Mr. Charles seems to care for me. I trust him," Samuel responded.

"There you go. Go! Go back there, wake up, and save our culture and the young generation. My wolf and my eagle are your helpers," Grandpa Jimmy said as he touched Samuel's head.

There was a very bright light, and Samuel felt like he was soaring, accelerating with maximum speed, and he opened his eyes. He was wondering where he was.

He slowly opened his eyes and wiggled his fingers.

"He's back! He's awake! Nurse! Nurse!" Annie called out.

"Where am I?" Samuel uttered.

He was at St. Mary's Hospital in the intensive care unit. Doctors thought it would take months before he woke up from his comatose condition.

Samuel woke up in the hospital with an invigorated spirit. Slowly opening his eyes, he first saw bright images that were becoming vivid. His mother was smiling with teary eyes and could not hide her worry. Due to the precautions of the doctor, she was hesitant to hug Samuel. But no doctor's advice is more powerful than a mother's love for her son, so she went and embraced Samuel anyway. Samuel also recognized his father, his three sisters, and his foster mom, Twyla. He was trying to think about the event. On his visitors' faces were traces of happiness, but they were all teary while smiling. They were sick with worry.

"What happened?" he asked.

"You were asleep for almost three months." Liza, his sister, explained that Manser had knocked him out during the ice fishing trip. Annie, Mina, and Liza took turns trying to recall what had happened during the ice fishing trip.

"You were like a total idiot, standing almost in the centre of the slope. Manser took that chance to get you," Mina said. Her tone was like that of an older sister, implying that it was his fault.

"Stop that!" Liza warned Mina. "Samuel, you were awesome and brave for helping the supervisors make sure that everyone was safe during the ice fishing trip. Don't worry. You're safe now, and you're back," Liza added.

"We're glad you're awake now, Samuel," Twyla said, relieved. She had been looking after Samuel since he was seven years old. She treated Samuel as her son.

Samuel closed his eyes and recalled what had happened during that day. He had a flashback. After he fell on the ground, a bright light came to rescue him, and he woke up in a very peaceful place.

"I thought it was real," Samuel whispered, feeling disappointed.

"Awoooooooooo!"

"Eeeiiiing!"

He could not get up yet, due to all the gadgets attached to his body. He glanced at the open window, and he could see the bald eagle on a branch of the spruce tree in the hospital's compound. He felt that the bird had been there for a long time, watching him. The gray wolf was under the tree. Samuel wondered why there was a wild animal on the loose in the middle of the day. Was it coincidental that both the eagle and the wolf were appearing to him at the same time?

"It's real...it's real!" Samuel happily blurted out.

"What's real?" everyone wondered.

Samuel shared his dream: that he had talked to their grandpa, and he was the one who had sent him back to earth. They tried to accompany Samuel to the washroom, but he said he was okay. They wondered how Samuel could easily walk even though he had not eaten, or drank any water, for three months.

Samuel was kept in the hospital for five more days to recuperate. During those days, he was happy that his family was beside him. He knew that his parents loved him. They just couldn't stay sober so that the children could go back to their house again. He liked Twyla, but there was no place like home, and you should be with your birth parents. Samuel hoped that he could go back to his birth parents.

"Mom...Dad, are you are taking me home?" he asked.

"You are still going to Twyla's home, son. I hope you understand," his parents explained.

Samuel was speechless. He felt sad because his parents couldn't stay sober. He did not utter a word, but his parents knew that he wanted to go back home to live with them. His parents wanted Samuel to be successful. They could not give him that dream if they kept drinking.

The family took Samuel back to the reserve, to his foster home. Everyone in the house was teasing him instead of supporting him about what had happened. He wondered why, this time, he never felt anything about their teasing. Before, he would react quickly and cry, but this time, he felt differently. There was an inner strength that was working inside him.

"Hello, guys!" he greeted them. "I will just rest in my room."

Everyone was wondering why he had only responded like that. "That was not like Samuel," they said. "He's supposed to cry and weep and just stay in his room. That was the total opposite." They looked at one another, and then they let out a loud laugh.

"Hahahahahahaha!"

"Who is he? A ghost?" Garrett laughed.

In his room, Samuel checked himself in the mirror. He took off his glasses, and there was no difference. Samuel could see clearly without his glasses. He took off his shirt and observed his body. Before, Samuel hadn't noticed any bicep muscles, but now Samuel could feel a big difference. He had bigger bicep muscles, and he had agility. He tried doing a handstand.

"Wow!"

He tried to do push-ups, and he did them quickly. He felt like he would have to do a million reps to exhaust the energy that he was exuding at that moment. His imagination started to spark. He opened the window in his room. He tried to do it quietly to not get any extra attention from the people down in the living room who was watching *The Walking Dead*. From the window, he looked down, and it was quite a height. Samuel moved back to his door, and then he ran towards the window and jumped headfirst, diving as he would into a pool. He cleared the window like a tiger jumping through a circle of fire. Samuel landed on the ground smoothly. Nobody noticed that he was out of the house. Samuel ran like the wind towards Abbey Road to visit the sledding area at Remba Lake once again. The gray wolf and the bald eagle were there, watching and providing him with spiritual strength that he had never had before. The eagle and the wolf, Samuel's spirit guides, sent him energy and inner strength. This feeling made him go faster, like a gazelle running through the woods. He never got tired from running. It was at least ten kilometres from the community to Remba Lake, but it was nothing to him. Watching the birds flying overhead, looking for a chance for any food, entertained him, and he contemplated his second life.

CHAPTER 4

The New Samuel

Samuel woke up early, showing his excitement about going back to school after being out for almost three months. One more month and school would be over. He had lots of work to catch up on. Twyla, his foster mom, was amazed at how well Samuel behaved on that morning. She did not need to go to his room and pull him out of bed. Most of the time, it would be a "dragging moment" every Monday since Samuel did not want to go to school. He had always been feeling tired because of playing online games the whole night. This time, it was a different story. Samuel had only spent one to two hours playing them. Twyla saw him grab his book and read for about fifteen minutes. He seemed so happy and was smiling at them. It was impressive to see the transformation in Samuel. Twyla pretended that she did not notice anything. She just let the change unfold as it was, and she saw that it was flourishing. Samuel did not have to wait for her to tell him what to do; instead, he was the one offering her breakfast. The impact of the ice sledding incident must have had some effect on Samuel. It must have struck a brain wire and made it function to its fullest as some other geniuses have after such an unexpected event.

"Let's go, Liza, Mina, Annie...the bus is here," Samuel said in an encouraging voice. His sisters were the ones waiting for his lead now. The sisters just looked at each other, wondering what was going on with Samuel. They preferred not to say it. There was a time when the bus, after ten minutes, would just leave them behind because they were so slow. The bus driver expected everyone to be at their pick-up spot to ensure that all students would arrive at school on time. The school was within walking distance, so sometimes they ended up walking to school or not going to school because they didn't like to walk. They would just wait for the lunchtime bus run.

"Good morning, Fina!" Samuel greeted the bus driver.

"Hey, Samuel, that's a new one. Welcome back!" the bus driver greeted in return.

Fina was not used to greeting the students. She was a strict bus driver and had to yell because the students were so loud. They could not sit still. Most of the time, the little children's parents were complaining because of bullies on the bus. Even though there was a supervisor, children would always be children. The supervisor still prompted them to sit down. Some students were so challenging, but others were naturally well-behaved. The school didn't condone bullies on the bus, but it was just another way of staying at home to play video games if they got suspended. One time, I needed to go on the bus to check on slashed bus seats, two of which were new. Not even one student would tell who did the damage. Witnesses didn't want to come forward because they knew the repercussions if they reported them.

Samuel sat quietly in his usual seat with his sisters. All eyes focused on him, and the other children started laughing. Samuel didn't want to be laughed at anymore.

"Wake up, Samuel! Wake up!" they teased him.

He did not say anything. He was immune to being the centre of joking and teasing. He completely ignored them. Bullies feast on weaker kids, and they feel delighted when they can get into the heads of the ones they target.

"Be quiet and stop teasing him! Be nice," Liza said, defending her brother.

Samuel completely ignored them and remained calm. He was not going to be affected by the teasing. To him, it was nothing, but it had to stop. Other children were subject to ridicule, and they were not resilient enough to bounce back. There were children of school age at home, scared to go to school because of this problem. Parents didn't even want their children on the bus. Sometimes other children were so rough, and they had no control over their behaviour. Samuel was aware of those bullies on the bus, and he had a plan. He needed to end this crap so that more children could go to school and learn.

"Wake up, Samuel; wake up! Hahahahahahaha!" The teasing continued.

Samuel stood up and told them, "I'm awake now, and I will tell you that there's a lot more coming." Samuel expressed himself for the first time.

"Good job, Samuel!" Fina said.

Fina was aware that Samuel had not been standing up for himself. It was the first time she had seen a student stand up against bullies on the bus. This event was a good sign. Then Samuel sat down quietly. Manser was on the bus at that time, and he was busy stirring up all the commotions on the bus. Manser was the most prominent bus bully. He got up and directly rushed over to where Samuel sat.

"What did you say?" He was trying to scare Samuel with a clenched fist, and he started to throw a punch.

Samuel did not blink or anything, and he was not scared. He knew that the punch would never reach him.

Intimidation and scaring children were always the bullies' strategy, but it was not working on Samuel at the moment.

"Sit down, Manser!" Fina yelled.

Manser looked at Fina with a smile and then warned Samuel. "See you at school!" Manser threatened.

No one cared about what had happened. Samuel had ignored him and hadn't even twitched. Johnny noticed that Manser had just got ditched.

"Samuel did not even show that he was scared of you," he taunted Manser.

Some students liked to goad the instigator. They wanted to see real action.

"I will get him at school, that f*****g b***h!" Manser was furious.

Not getting what they want makes a bully even more frustrated. They feed on how much they intimidate and scare people. It makes them feel superior and powerful. Manser thought about how Samuel had reacted. He saw Samuel never showed emotion. But how come? Manser wanted to find out why Samuel had not even shown any sign of being afraid. Samuel felt good, and he was not even bothered by how Manser had treated him on the bus. The children noticed too that Samuel was not scared of him anymore. They used to see him cry like a baby all the time. This bullying was the reason that he was sometimes not even motivated to go to school. Now, it was different. Samuel had found new energy and inspiration, which would make the bus, the school, and even the community better. It had to change.

"Did you see that? Manser was confused. He did not do anything to me. When someone tries to scare you, don't show them that you are scared. Stand up against them, or ignore them, and share with adults that someone is bothering you. You are all strong. Find that strength inside you, and stop fooling around on the bus; always behave." Samuel had the power to follow up on what had happened.

Fina was happy. That was something from a budding young person. The school needed more student leaders who were willing to apply what they learned in school. The future of the

Dahmedeh First Nation relied on them and the foundation of cultural knowledge that they would learn from home and the school.

"Welcome back, Samuel." Everyone in the school was happy to welcome Samuel back. They knew what had happened, and they still remembered why they had gone home early. They also knew that it was Manser's doing, but they got used to it. The most important thing was that Samuel was back, and he was alive.

The great thing about the Dahmedeh Community School is the camaraderie. All staff and students are families unless they do not want to participate in everyone's progress every day. Every day brings excitement and surprises. The behaviour of children is like a roller coaster. There will always be a rocky road, but with the firm will and concerted effort of staff and parents, young people will turn into young leaders, and they will realize that when the time comes.

"Thank you," Samuel said as he smiled back at them. He immediately went to his classroom.

"Samuel, welcome back!" Mr. Parson greeted him with a smile. He approached Samuel to hug him.

Samuel stepped back a bit. "Just shake a hand, Mr. Parson." He was putting his right hand out simultaneously.

Samuel was not used to hugging. Maybe he got that from being away from his biological mother. His condition also made him not used to touching.

"Samuel, did you work out when you were asleep?" Mr. Parson wondered. He felt the strength of Samuel's hand. "You seem so sturdy," Mr. Parson said. Shaking hands demonstrates respect. I always tensed my hand when I shook hands with Mr. Lorenzo because he squeezed my hand every time we shook hands. A rough palm shows that one is a hard worker and used to holding tools all the time. That was Mr. Lorenzo. It was like we always had an arm wrestle every time we shook hands.

Samuel noticed it too. He could feel that the hand of Mr. Parson was soft and had no strength at all. It was like shaking a girl's hand; it was so smooth. Samuel wondered why, but he felt more potent than usual. He felt like he needed to burn a lot of energy. Maybe it came from not doing anything for three months. Perhaps he had stored lots of strength.

"No, Mr. Parson. Maybe it was the food they gave me at the hospital," he said jokingly.

"So, Mr. Parson, what are we going to learn today?" he added. Mr. Parson was excited. Samuel had never asked about a lesson before.

Samuel started to work on whatever lessons he had missed during his absence. He would ask Mr. Parson for help whenever he didn't understand specific terms and problems. Mr. Parson was great at piling up all the worksheets that Samuel needed to catch up on. Other students seemed to understand and sympathize with Samuel's condition. Only Manser never stopped thinking mischievously about how to get him one more time.

During recess, Samuel went to visit Mr. Charles.

"Rhoze, can I see Mr. Charles?" he politely asked.

"Good morning, Samuel. It's nice to see you back!" Rhoze was so welcoming. She was the school secretary for the entire K–12 program. Being alone at the front desk was quite a challenge; however, Rhoze persevered and loved her job. Students and staff loved her kindness and compassion. She was the workhorse of the school.

Rhoze checked to see if Mr. Charles was busy. His office was always open to everyone. He only closed the door when he was in a confidential meeting.

"You can go in now, Samuel. He's waiting for you."

Samuel thanked Rhoze and happily went into Mr. Charles' office.

"Samuel, it's nice to see you back. When I heard the news that you were back, I was so excited to come and see you, but my phone keeps ringing. As you know, it's Monday. Thank you for taking the initiative to see me." Mr. Charles welcomed Samuel on his first day back since being in a comatose state.

"What a strong hand grip!" Mr. Charles noticed the strength of Samuel's hand when he shook it.

"I don't know, Mr. Charles. I feel like I'm so strong!" Samuel chuckled.

Mr. Charles was delighted with what he heard. He was a very sports-minded person, and he liked healthy students. Strong athletes bring honour to the school and the community as well.

"What's the plan, Samuel? How do you feel?" Mr. Charles was curious.

"Mr. Charles, I want to catch up on my studies, and I also would like to do more sports, but I would like to start by learning some self-defense moves from you." Samuel enthusiastically shared his thoughts with Mr. Charles.

Mr. Charles was happy with what he heard from Samuel. He had been dreaming of having at least one disciple to learn his martial arts skills. Back in the Philippines, he had a lot of students that won in the tournaments. It is a discipline that every individual should learn. There is lots of bullying and domestic violence because of a lack of discipline and knowledge to defend themselves from adversaries.

We tried to offer Introduction to Self-Defence as an option course, and there were six junior high school students enrolled. The first requirement was to bring their jogging pants. The six students struggled to get their suits. Mr. Charles was the one who brought jogging pants and lent them to the students. He taught them some calisthenics and started with stretch kicks. Suddenly, those students began to kick lockers and fool around, despite the tenets and expectations that they needed to keep the knowledge to themselves. They failed to follow, so Mr. Charles discontinued the program.

Samuel started to train with Mr. Charles at least three times a week after school. Mr. Charles was happy to share what he knew with a future defender of bullied young people.

CHAPTER 5

The Tests of Tenacity

Manser was antsy to get off the bus. He could not accept the fact that Samuel had just ignored him that way. Bullies are not happy when they can't find someone to bully, and Samuel had not given him that craving.

"I'll get you in the school!" Manser said, looking at Samuel sternly.

Samuel didn't give him any sign of emotion. He was thinking of different tactics to get back at Manser. He calmly got off the bus, and Manser was so mad about not getting his dose of bully medication. One could expect that this would not be a good day for teachers. The volcano inside him was about to erupt, and it was because he did not get into Samuel's bully zone. Manser knew he had many chances to get Samuel in the school: in the classroom, in the washroom, or the gym. He could choose any spot or just right in the large lunch area.

Manser never even considered any staff members. He was not scared of anybody. Manser wanted the school to suspend him. It would be a reward for him because he could stay home and play online games the whole day or week. He knew that his brother and his father were in and out of jail. The police recently arrested his dad for assaulting his mom, and his brother was spending six years at the High River Correctional Centre for stabbing his grandpa. Just imagine hurting your grandpa, who looked after and raised you. That was elder abuse. His grandpa could not give him money because his pension cheque never came yet, and Manser could not even understand that. The poor older man should have disciplined his grandson when he was young. Manser was on his way to following the path of his father and brother. What would be the proper antidote for this contagious social sickness?

"Out of my way!" Manser bumped Samuel back when he got off the bus. Samuel showed no reaction at all. He knew that he had defeated Manser psychologically. Samuel knew that Manser would come his way, but that was just a small problem to deal with in the meantime. In his ears, he could hear the howling of the wolf and the screeching of the eagle. The presence of his spirit guides gave him the courage to look beyond his fear. Samuel knew that he had a source of power and strength, and he greeted everyone with a smile.

"Samuel, welcome back. We're delighted to see you back." Supervisors greeted him.

" Thank you." Samuel slightly smiled.

Mr. Charles was also at the door welcoming the children. "Welcome, children. How are you this morning?"

"Oh, Samuel, welcome back. I missed your drawing."

"Don't worry, Mr. Charles, I will draw you a great one."

Mr. Charles noticed the enthusiasm in Samuel. He also noticed that Samuel had suddenly changed. Mr. Charles tried to hold Samuel's arm, and because the boy trusted him, he was free to touch him. "Samuel, what happened? Did you work out during your holidays?" Mr. Charles inquired. He could feel the extra energy in the hands of Samuel. Mr. Charles presumed that Samuel might even be more powerful than him. Mr. Charles did not say anything, but he was interested in the transformation in Samuel. He suffered because of bullies all the time, and he expected that Samuel might be in the office again later, reporting that Manser was bugging him. It might be interesting what that change would bring for Samuel.

The school always had breakfast ready for the students. This breakfast program was beneficial for the children. They learned and behaved better if they had something in their stomachs. Some children from the reserve communities did not have a proper breakfast because parents were not ready to give them food in the morning. They might still be sleeping, and others may not be sober enough to get up. Based on the previous anecdotal report, it was evident that the children were cooperative and willing to listen more if they were healthy and had breakfast.

Samuel was on his way back to his table with his pancake, egg, and a small glass of orange juice. Manser was ready with his set-up ambush. He intentionally extended his leg to trip him. To his surprise, Samuel just stepped over his leg as he expected the action. Samuel did not even look at Manser. He just continued walking towards his table. Manser was so angry. He could not do anything because supervisors were everywhere, and he also noticed, out of the corner of his eye, that Mr. Charles was looking at him. He pretended that nothing had happened. Manser knew that doing something stupid too early would make Mr. Charles send him home. He would not be able to get Samuel today. He also knew that in-school suspension meant lots of work and one-on-one supervision. This situation would spoil his plan for Samuel. "Lots of time; I'll get you inside the classroom," Manser whispered.

After "O Canada," all students started to head to their respective classrooms. Manser kept an eye on Samuel if he were to go to the washroom so that he would have the chance to bully him. Unfortunately, Samuel went straight to their classroom.

"Good morning...good morning!" He was happy to be back in his class after three months in the hospital. He checked his binder, and he found the pile of unfinished work. Without a prompt, Samuel started to work on his assignments. All his classmates barely noticed the change in him because they were all busy goofing around. That was the trend in that Grade 7 class: Students ignored teachers and just went about their own business. They were waiting for a more stringent teacher to tell them sternly and precisely what to do. Sometimes students knew if the teacher had low expectations, and they would not care. They knew that they struggled so much, so their defense mechanism was a "we failed anyway" attitude. It is a self-fulfilling prophecy, believing that they would just wait for social assistance support when they were eighteen years old.

"Good job, Samuel!" Mr. Parson said as he noticed his initiative. He had already finished five assignments when the teacher came and checked attendance. Mr. Parson had noticed

Samuel every day as the most behaved and quietest boy in the class. If he did not see Samuel, he would search in the cupboard, locker, or washroom. Mr. Parson would know what had happened. The reason could be because of something at home or because Manser and his gang of bullies had started to bother him. This time, it was a different Samuel that Mr. Parson saw in the class. Samuel never asked for any help from anybody. He was so independent and just worked quietly away at his pile of assignments. Mr. Parson let Samuel know that service was always available. He even offered Samuel that he could stay after school for extra support.

"I'm fine, Mr. Parson. Thank you!" Samuel was so polite.

Mr. Parson thought that this might be an after-effect of Samuel having been comatose. Mr. Parson wanted to commend Samuel for his attitude in the morning; notably, he had just got back after three months.

"Class, I would like you to welcome Samuel. We missed him, and I hope that you will help him catch up with his lessons if he asks for help," said Mr. Parson.

"He can do it. He is a very smart a**." Manser started it again. Samuel just smiled. He did not react or anything, and everybody noticed that.

"Yes, I can do it. As Manser said, I'm like him: a smart a**!" Samuel joked around.

"F*** y**!" I will get you. You'll see." Manser was mad again. He noticed that Samuel was not scared of him anymore.

"That's enough, Manser. Just be happy that Samuel is back," Mr. Parson interrupted.

The class continued to be rowdy. Others were ready to listen, but others kept talking. This type of incident was not new to Samuel. He kept doing his work to catch up. He wanted to go to the Grade 8 class in September. As Mr. Parson was teaching math, Samuel stopped for a while and butted in sometimes when he knew the answer. Mr. Parson was pleased with how well Samuel was doing. He did not expect it from Samuel, but Samuel showed a student's attitude in a regular school.

"Tyrone, Tyrone!" Samuel whispered to call Tyrone's attention, another quiet boy in his class who was also subject to bullying.

Tyrone slowly looked at Samuel and smiled. Tyrone was also diagnosed with FASD and delayed response, but if you gave him enough time to process, he would give you the exact answer you needed. Both of them were quiet boys in the class and the most targeted by the school's bullies. No one saw the abilities of these boys yet, because they had no chance to exhibit any. They were so scared to show what they knew.

"How are you, Samuel? Happy to see you back!" Tyrone responded.

Ringgggggggg! The bell went for the physical education period. That was the most awaited moment by Manser, to get Samuel. Usually, Samuel would just sit in the bleachers and watch, or he would plead with the teacher to have a zombie game. If the teacher disagreed, then he would leave the gym or go to the washroom and cry. Manser knew all those situations, and if one of those situations arose, surely he would be able to get Samuel.

Students slowly passed their work and waited for Mr. Parson to ask them to line up. Students had learned the routine that the teacher had set during the first week of school. They should have got it by now since it was June. Others did not understand yet, especially Manser's group. Mr. Parson needed to yell at the top of his lungs before he could get those boys to fall in line. Samuel was in front already, behind Tyrone. They were planning to stay after school and see Mr. Charles. Samuel wanted Tyrone to come with him. Usually, Tyrone's grandma picked them up, but Samuel said they would ask Mr. Charles to drive them home.

"I just want to ask him something, and I would like you to come with me," Samuel explained.

It was not hard to convince Tyrone. He also liked to spend some time with Samuel. He was the only close friend he had. When Samuel was absent for three months, no one wanted to play with him. He was alone. He was too slow for the other boys.

"Get out of my way!" Manser inserted himself in the line between Samuel and Tyrone.

"Ouch!" Tyrone complained and quickly pushed Manser towards Samuel. Tyrone was as big as him. He had the strength to topple Manser down, but he was too scared to fight. He removed himself from the line, went to the back of the classroom, and started crying. Manser tried to grab Samuel while falling intentionally, but Samuel quickly avoided him, so Manser crashed to the floor. He got up immediately and looked for Tyrone, but Tyrone was not in the line anymore. Samuel just ignored him and pretended that nothing had happened, but the whole class laughed at Manser. Manser looked around and caught Tyrone smiling. He went to him and threw a punch. Samuel quickly pulled Tyrone to the side, and Manser hit the whiteboard hard.

"Ahhhhhh! My hand, my hand," Manser cried.

Nobody said anything, but everyone was probably thinking, "Good for you, Mr. Bully."

"It's because of you, Samuel. You should die and never come back to class!" Manser shouted.

"Stop it now," Mr. Parson said. He asked Klay, his EA, to take Manser down to the office for first aid. They put an icepack on his hand, and Jelly, the liaison officer, checked his hand if she should take him to the clinic to see if there was a fracture. Manser would not stop swearing. He was furious with Samuel, and he was blaming him for everything. Jelly phoned Manser's grandma to let her know what had happened. She went to Mr. Parson's class to remind him about the incident report. Writing incident reports consumed most of the teachers' time, especially during the transition period, where they had the chance to fool around. Teachers and EAs should always be proactive to avoid such an accident. Manser went to the clinic, and the nurse said it was just a bruise to the muscle.

"It is just a bruise. You don't have to worry," the medical aide said.

The nurse cleared Manser to go back to school after applying some kind of ointment for pain. The pain was supposed to go away soon, but it took a while. Manser needed to nurse it at least every couple of hours.

"I will get him; I will get him," Manser said, referring to Samuel. He would not accept that Samuel had hurt him without even engaging.

"I will see how tough he is. I will have my time," Manser said to himself.

During gym time, the students had fun playing tag.

"You never had a chance to be IT yet, Samuel," Emerson shouted. "What happened to you? Before, you couldn't even run fast."

It was June and track and field season, so the class was usually outside playing: running, playing tag, jumping, throwing—any games that incorporated running. Mr. Parson liked physical education time because he was a multi-skilled player of any kind.

The tag was the favourite game of the children. Samuel, himself, always suggested freeze tag when Mr. Parson would say, "It's a free choice for a fun game today!"

So, Samuel immediately shouted, "Freeze Tag!" Everyone agreed because they liked tag, primarily when Mr. Parson chased them.

"Let's jog around the school fence to build your stamina. Remember, it is not a race, so don't run. Just jog or walk. After that, we can play softball," Mr. Parson said.

The whole class started jogging. Most of the girls just strolled and talked. Samuel asked Tyrone to follow him, and the two boys began racing ahead of the crowd. Tyrone was smiling, jogging beside Samuel. They had never done this together. They were both lazy, but with the different perspectives that Samuel had brought back since his first day from his three-month absence, it was contagious. Tyrone felt intense energy when he was with Samuel. They both started speeding up. The jogging turned into a fun run. Mr. Parson was happy to see the two slow boys leading the pack with a lively and energetic stride. After a round, Tyrone was tired, so he decided to sit down. Samuel still had enough energy and ran another lap. He ran faster than usual, and he even finished the lap before the class.

"That was awesome, Samuel. You're a natural runner!" Mr. Parson congratulated him.

After the lap, the class played softball as planned. Samuel stayed on second base. He did not know how to play softball yet. He was scared even to hit the ball before, but now he volunteered to be on first base. Darian, a bigger boy in his class, volunteered to be the pitcher. Other students grabbed their gloves and spread out in the diamond. Students in the Dahmedeh Community School had not experienced playing competitive softball yet. It was just an exposure to the game. Mr. Parson was the first batter to show the students how to hit the ball accurately. It was a slow-pitch style first, as you throw the ball slowly with an arc. Mr. Parson hit the ball so hard that it was a home run. It was out of the diamond, and the ball flew out to the centre field. Samuel saw the ball, and without hesitation, he ran and chased it, past the centre fielder. Samuel was under the ball in just the blink of an eye, waiting for it to fall into his glove.

BOOOOOOM! Samuel caught the ball, and everyone was celebrating and shouting. They could not believe that Samuel had done that. Mr. Parson could not believe it either. He hit the ball as an adult to impress the students, but he was embarrassed because Samuel had caught it, and his home run did not count. The game continued, and it was Samuel's turn. He had never hit a ball before. He was a little bit nervous, but he was confident that he could hit the ball. Mr. Parson volunteered to be the pitcher so that the students would have a fair chance of hitting the ball. When he pitched the ball to Samuel, he purposely put some spins on it so that Samuel would miss it. To his surprise, Samuel swung his bat and hit the ball in the right spot.

"WOW!" everyone exclaimed in amazement. The ball flew outside the diamond for a home run.

"HOME RUN Samuel, go!" Everyone urged him to run fast. Samuel ran excitedly around the bases. It was his first hit, and it was also a home run. It was like a double treat ice cream with extra flavour. Mr. Parson and everyone else could not believe it. Samuel's classmates were just so happy for him. They had never before seen those things that Samuel could do. Samuel had woke up as a different Samuel. Those boys would not even envy Samuel because they were playing games. Children forget to do bad stuff when they are preoccupied with activities. They were just happy; there was a teacher spending quality playtime with them. Of course, other students wanted to hit a home run, too, so they wanted to be the batter now. They wanted to experience how Samuel felt when he hit that ball so hard and got a home run. Samuel felt like he was on cloud nine. The eagle was in the sky, and the howling of his wolf from afar was a message to Samuel. "Thank you, Grandpa!" Samuel whispered.

CHAPTER 6

The Encounter with Lyle

Another developing sport at Dahmedeh Community School is basketball. Mr. Charles was good at it. Nobody on the team could beat him one-on-one. He was a coach and a referee. They always won a medal in the Developing Basketball League Division throughout the school division.

Students spend their time indoors during lunchtime, and most of them choose to be in the gym. Others are in the computer laboratories, in the library, in the classrooms, or just in the hallway.

"Five free throws in a row; that's impressive, Lyle," Mr. Charles excitedly praised Lyle.

It was pouring rain outside; that was why the students had indoor recess. Junior high and senior high school students stayed in the gym, and the elementary students were in the computer laboratories, library, and in their classrooms. In the gym, Mr. Charles was supervising and keeping an eye on those boisterous students that would take the chance to bully students. Most of the students grabbed, bounced, and shot balls; others were just spectators, sitting in the bleachers or on the stage, on their phones. Others were in and out of the gym, but students were just bored, waiting for the bell to go because they had stricter supervisors.

The praise gave Lyle even more self-confidence to challenge Mr. Charles to play basketball. No one had ever beaten Mr. Charles at one-on-one yet. He was short—maybe five foot six inches tall—but he was tricky and legit at playing basketball. He played good basketball and liked to challenge all the high school players one-on-one, but no one had succeeded yet.

"Mr. Charles, let's play one-on-one basketball; I can easily beat you," Lyle challenged.

Lyle is a six-foot-two big boy who was once in the Special Education class. He always underestimated the people around him because of his size. Lyle is tall but uncoordinated. He could shoot the ball ten times before scoring, while Mr. Charles could score with his eyes closed. What he just did today may be a fluke, but he had convinced himself that because he made five straight throws, he was now a professional basketball player. That was only shooting, and it might not be consistent. How about dribbling? If a player doesn't have enough dribbling skills, he can quickly lose the ball, or he can fumble and lose the ball. Players will struggle to play if they don't have dribbling skills.

"Sorry, Lyle. There are lots of students in the gym, and I'm the only supervisor here," Mr. Charles apologized.

Samuel was aware of the conversation. He knew that Lyle would not take no for an answer. Samuel helped out with putting all the equipment away. Children usually just left the stuff on the floor.

"Come on, Mr. Charles. I want to beat you at basketball," Lyle insisted.

Prrrtttt! Prrrt! Prrrrt! whistled Mr. Charles.

Three blasts of the whistle meant that it was time to go back to the classroom. Mr. Charles ignored the escalating behaviour of Lyle. He instructed him to put all the equipment back in the equipment room. Students followed at once, but Lyle refused to comply. He was still shooting hoops.

"Alright, the gym is closed! Lyle, lunch break is over; you have two minutes to report to your class," Mr. Charles directed Lyle.

Usually, when students with challenging behaviour knew their parameters, they tended to cooperate and follow. Samuel was also watching. He knew that if Mr. Charles needed help, he could quickly provide a hand.

Lyle struggled to follow instructions once he fixated on what he was asking.

"But I am still playing."

"Recess is over. It's time to report to your class," Mr. Charles directed.

After a long argument, Lyle threw the ball hard at Samuel. But Samuel caught it quickly.

Lyle stormed out of the gym, kicking the door hard. At that time, Mr. Parson had been inserting his gym key, so he got hit in the head, and Lyle bumped into him. Mr. Parson was a little dizzy. Mr. Charles drove him to the nurse's station for concussion protocol.

Lyle went straight to the washroom and washed his face.

Samuel also went to the washroom, pretending to use it.

"You little sh**, make sure you are not in my way. I can break you easily," Lyle threatened Samuel.

Samuel was calm and did not say anything. He just looked at Lyle coldly.

Lyle rushed back to his classroom and had not gotten himself into the groove yet. He was still pouting, with clenched fists. Letting go was hard for him. He refused to follow, looked upset and frustrated. He was angry and was looking at Mr. Charles. Mr. Charles had been standing at the front of the class for ten minutes. He could not start his math PowerPoint presentation.

Like in elementary school, most high school students behave like little kids. They don't settle immediately and start paying attention to the teacher. The teacher needs to do a lot of prompting before students will settle down.

"I could shove your head in the computer right now," Lyle angrily said. For some reason, Lyle had carried his anger into the classroom. He could not accept that Mr. Charles had not taken his challenge.

"Let him teach!" Julia exclaimed. The girls in the classroom wanted to learn. Most of the boys did not want to study, and they were just occupying the teacher's time. It was a challenge for Mr. Charles to get his students into an actual grade level. There were lots of accommodations and differentiation, and this was a great example.

Lyle was sitting beside Byron, the lad who used to beat him when they were just little boys.

One summer, Mr. Charles watched from the window of his teacher's unit, which overlooked the vast space where the boys always hung out when they were biking. He heard a group of young boys yelling and cheering. A bigger boy was on the ground, and a little boy was kicking him repeatedly. He went to check who he was. The boys ran away, but from afar, he recognized Byron as the one kicking the boy on the ground, and when he got to the place, he saw that it was Lyle.

Mr. Charles was conscientious. He observed the mood of the class. He knew that Byron could grab Lyle right away and wrestle him to the ground. But no, that would be too violent inside the class. He had other ways to handle things like this, especially with these big boys.

"Is something bothering you, Lyle?" Mr. Charles inquired.

"I said I could shove your head in the computer right now!" Lyle repeated.

"Oh," Mr. Charles answered calmly.

"Let's fight. Let's box. Let's see who is powerful!" Lyle said, with his challenging voice.

"Oh, I see," Mr. Charles responded calmly. "Get up and ask Mr. Green if he has a pair of boxing gloves. We might get hurt," Mr. Charles said in a very calm voice.

Lyle got up and walked out the door. "Come here now!" said Lyle, with a persistent voice.

"Nope; go to Mr. Green's office and ask him if he has gloves," Mr. Charles insisted.

After Lyle left the classroom, Mr. Charles closed the door and instructed the students not to open it for safety reasons. He pulled out his cellphone and called the principal's office.

"Can you call a cop for me? Lyle is too big for me to deal with." Mr. Charles requested the police to come.

Mr. Charles was expecting a commotion in the hallway, and he heard a brief noise. He knew that someone was on the way, and Lyle might have just smacked them to death.

PAK! PAK! PAK!

The students went out and saw Lyle on the floor, unconscious. They had just heard the noise, and there he was, lying on the floor. No one saw anybody.

Mr. Charles requested Wally to check the camera. The school has cameras due to break and entries and other unforeseen incidents like this.

From what had happened in the gym, Samuel already knew what was going to happen. Samuel had not gone to his class right away; instead, he waited and watched from outside, in the hallway, to keep an eye on Mr. Charles. He did not fail.

"You won't believe this, Mr. Charles," Wally said in amazement.

The camera showed that Samuel was walking towards Mr. Charles' classroom when Lyle tried to push him against the wall.

"Get out of my way, you little freak!"

"Watch yourself! Grow up!" Samuel parried Lyle's hands and smacked him on the back of his head. Lyle fell to the floor unconscious.

Wally and Mr. Charles could not believe what they saw. Samuel was not big enough to parry the force of an angry boy, but he just did it like nothing. He was supposed to be scared because Lyle was twice his size. His aura was beaming, and he seemed healthy.

Mr. Charles and Wally carried Lyle into the principal's office. They waited until he regained consciousness.

"It is not okay to challenge your teacher, Lyle," Constable Warman cautioned Lyle.

Constable Warman was the designated police officer for the

school. He conducted school children's programs to ensure that they would not break the law when they turned thirteen. Usually, before they reached that age, youth would experience being in jail and would face juvenile court. That would be Lyle's case if he continued exhibiting violent behaviour, especially with professional people.

Lyle apologized to Mr. Charles. He did not even remember that Samuel had given him the smack on the head.

Children with a condition like Lyle's could not retain anything. They would quickly forget and could not rationalize what they did. They would fixate on something, and then it was a challenge to get over it. After Lyle made his apology, it was like nothing had happened. He did not hold any grudges and did not even find out why he was unconscious on the floor.

Students would have expected that Mr. Charles would not come back for the next school year due to Lyle's incident. They understood the cause of the fast turnover of staff. Students like Lyle scared them off. They were lucky if they stayed until June and just finished their contract.

Students were aware that Mr. Charles is a strict teacher. He would not easily give in to a little incident like this. Mr. Charles knew that nobody got hurt, and Samuel was the new hero, without anyone even noticing. Still, Mr. Charles knew about Samuel's extraordinary strength since he had come out of the comatose state.

"Samuel, can I have a word with you?" Mr. Charles asked.

Samuel explained how he got the courage up to meet Lyle.

"I just felt that deep inside me, I was stronger than Lyle. There is a little boy inside him, and I have received humungous courage, acquired from the spirit of our ancestors. They told me to clean up this community and ensure that our young people retain and practice our culture."

Samuel also explained that Lyle was scared. He could feel the insecurity and challenges he was experiencing. His brain was not fully developed, and some functions could not correctly perceive the need to be regulated. Evil spirits can easily manipulate weak minds. Lyle was fragile, and hidden energy that a human could not imagine could easily influence him. Lyle's occurrence of behaviour was not unusual. He was of the mindset that he could conquer anything. With his mental state—being a child in a large frame—he would most likely behave irrationally.

As a teacher of physical education, I experienced working with Lyle on a one-on-one basis. He was in a Special Education class and was exceptionally smart in math. He rushed to finish all his worksheets to spend extra time in the gym. He liked to run with the soccer ball and showed me several kicking tricks. I wondered where he got the method from, but of course, if he had a vast flat-screen TV at home, he could always imitate the professional European soccer players' moves with a subscription to a sports channel. Young people nowadays are great imitators. Adults cannot keep abreast of these things in spending lots of time in front of screens.

Lyle was always apologetic. The staff just needed to understand the situation and avoid personalizing to serve the children in their best interest further.

CHAPTER 7

Gabu and Aiden's Brawl

"**D**o you think you're better than me?" Gabu pointed at Aiden and got closer, and then repeatedly poked him on his chest with his finger.

Mr. Charles was holding the basketball and was trying to convince players to play. There were eight at the court's centre, while others were just standing or sitting in the bleachers. They were waiting for an action to occur.

Aiden and Gabu both played basketball better than the other boys at Dahmedeh Community School. Aiden stood six foot flat, and Gabu stood at five foot eight inches. Both still need to be exposed to more scrimmages to develop their skills.

"Come on, guys, let's play some hoops!" he invited the students. He was aware of the situation in progress.

Samuel sensed trouble in the gym. "Mr. Parson, can I go to the washroom, please?" he asked.

As Mr. Charles approached the group of boys, Aiden punched Gabu twice in his face.

UM! UM! Aiden threw punches.

"WHOOWAAAAAH!" Gabu grabbed a broom and broke its handle for a weapon.

"Fight! Fight! Fight!" Students in the bleachers were cheering and recording the fight.

Mr. Charles quickly stayed between the two big boys to separate them.

"Come on, let's see how tough you are!" Gabu was attacking Aiden.

"I need help; I need help!" Mr. Charles shouted.

Samuel was right on time. He grabbed Aiden and pulled him to the side. He could not attack any further. Nobody dared to help stop him from attacking. Samuel showed his strength and bravery one more time. Other students did not utter a word, and to their surprise, a grade-7 boy stepped up to help Mr. Charles. Mr. Salko, a six-foot-four gym assistant, was stunned as he watched from the side and was in shock when the big fight broke out. But Samuel wrestled Aiden until he didn't resist anymore.

Everyone knew that Gabu was a gangster and a big bully. He intimidated everybody but could not fight with his bare hands. One time, I witnessed when Kendra and Cathy had pissed him off. He could not resist the two girls; instead, he grabbed a pair of scissors and chased them while crying.

Gabu also was showing some learning disability. His muscles were huge, and he could lift 240-pound weights, but his emotions and way of thinking were that of a seven-year-old boy.

On Tuesday morning, he was late to class—around ten o'-clock—and his classmates were already on their next subject in the science laboratory. He kicked the chair and seemed upset instead of greeting Mr. Charles.

"Can we go out and brawl?" Gabu challenged Mr. Charles.

"What are you thinking?" Mr. Charles said. "Let's check the weight room and hit the punching bag instead."

Mr. Charles was very good at redirecting the attention of angry youth. He knew what battles to pick.

Aiden was a quiet boy who loved playing basketball. He could leap high. With his six-foot height, he could dunk the ball. If he worked harder on his vertical jump, this boy could be a Dwight Howard type player. He was also a straight forward young lad. In his English language art class, he told his teacher that he did not like poetry. Mr. Charles chose a poem entitled "The Foul." He thought that Aiden would like it because it was about basketball. He was wrong.

"Why are we studying this? I would not be able to earn money with this shit," Aiden said.

He could not make any connection between this literary genre and the real world.

"You like songs, and poems are like songs," Mr. Charles explained while looking into Aiden's eyes.

"Why are you just staring at me? You're freaky," Aiden said.

It's part of their culture not to stare into the eyes of others. Still, in an ordinary world, one has to establish eye contact when communicating to show sincerity and honesty. By just looking into the eyes of someone, you can determine if they are telling the truth.

Gabu and Aiden resembled how Dahmedeh youth could be a strong force, especially on the athletic field. The school had a history of vital sports programs and healthy athletes a decade ago, but it suddenly changed due to a lack of dedicated teachers. Most great teachers left the community after several years of service.

Mr. Charles' first year of teaching was a great challenge. Students lacked exposure to sports and structured athletic programs. He took the risk of making a group of 14 boys attended Cross Country Divisionals at Sandy Lane School, a three-hour drive.

"Why are you taking those boys out of school? They will fight," Ms. Island said.

"These boys need someone to trust them, and they need to know what is out there," Mr. Charles said, defending why he was taking the boys out.

"Keep the phone number for the police. One time, those boys fought and ran away. Call us right away if something happens."

Ms. Island seemed very worried.

The boys arrived at the school early on the morning of the trip. They seemed all excited. For the first time in 10 years, they were going to participate in sports. I observed the rowdiness on the bus, but the behaviour was tolerable. I think a male coach can better relate to male athletes. We stopped at a store and observed how the boys behaved. Their behaviour was acceptable. No one attempted to shoplift as they had warned me. I just noticed that at a young age, these boys had cigarettes.

"How did you get a smoke?" I curiously asked.

"My mom," Lyndon said.

I learned that youth could access smokes and liquor in their homes. Maybe they were grabbing it without the knowledge or permission of their parents.

"Guys, what we need is to keep running and remember the trails," Samuel said to the boys.

It was excellent how the rest of the boys responded and listened to Samuel. It is human instinct to know who the alpha is. Being quiet demonstrated an agreement. The group of boys was quite intimidating; aside from the rugged behaviour, they wore all black.

After the registration, the group of runners did a walkthrough to familiarize themselves with the trails. There were some trail guides, but it was an advantage if a runner knew the path already. Mr. Charles assigned the boys based on their respective age categories. He did not precisely know the boys' capabilities when it came to running, but his experience as a sports coordinator in the Philippines gave him the confidence that some of the boys might make it. Dahmedeh had no public transportation, and youth were always biking or walking, so the training was regular with everyday life activities. Mr. Charles anticipated that Samuel would surely win. He was in the 4,000m category, while Gabu was in 5,000m, and Landon in 6,000m; and the rest of the runners were in 2000m and 3000m. Mr. Charles knew that Samuel would prevail.

The day was fantastic and bright. Runners needed to drink a lot of water on a hot, sunny day, perfect for runners.

"Screech, screech, screech." There were eagles in the sky.

"Awoooooooooooh!" The community heard the wolves howling in the air.

Sandy Lane had perfect cross country trails, used for both the summer and winter seasons. Thousands of runners from the different schools in the Mackenzie region attended the event. Mr. Charles did not know what to expect, but the game would undoubtedly be great exposure.

Mr. Charles waited at the finish line. The last stretch of the run was a five-hundred metre uphill run.

After several minutes, the runners began to arrive. It was a challenge on the hill, and runners tried their best to conquer it.

"What a run, Samuel! Good job!" Mr. Charles put his hand in the air, and Samuel enthusiastically tapped it.

Samuel finished his race in no time. It was like setting a new world record. The official world record for 4000m was less than 13 minutes, and Samuel finished close to that.

Colton and Ian came together for the 2000m. Mr. Charles was so happy to see that those boys had finished their race in no time. They were all sweaty and had big smiles on their faces.

"Excuse me, Mr. Charles," Mr. Thurston said.

Mr. Charles was smiling and laughing while talking to Mr. Thurston. Mr. Thurston informed him that Colton and Ian had taken a shortcut. The official disqualified them. I found it funny that these boys felt that they could take a shortcut.

The smiles on the faces of these young people demonstrated free souls out in the bush. They liked being out there, and they showed what they had. Almost all the runners had finished the race, but I wondered where Rex and Tyrone were.

Something was not right. Those boys should have been back by now. Mr. Charles asked Samuel to check on the boys.

He imitated the sound of the eagle: "Screech, screech, screech!"

He imitated the sound of the wolf. "Awoooooooh!"

Samuel ran back, deep down onto the trails. The wolf and eagle guided him to where they were. He ran, stopped, listened, and ran again. He knew exactly where the boys were.

"We were scared. We could not find our way back. We kept running fast; then, all of a sudden, everybody was gone," Rex said. Rex was not scared. He thought it was fun to get lost in the woods.

Tyrone was teary and looked tired. "You're crazy. What if a bear was chasing us? You never know."

"Come on, guys, you're safe now," Samuel said as he rescued his friends.

All the runners were in the gym, waiting for the final results.

"First place, 4000m, Samuel Yaluk, from Dahmedeh Community School," Mr. Thurston announced. Samuel excitedly went and got his gold medal. He was so happy and excited—it was his first medal, Mr. Charles' first medal as a coach, and the school's first gold medal. Mr. Charles had perceived that Samuel had that inner strength to excel in running. He felt that after having been comatose, Samuel was reborn as a strong boy.

"First place, 5000m, Gabu Thanianse, from Dahmedeh Community School," Mr. Thurston said into the microphone. Gabu smiled and went to get his medal. I felt and saw the pride on his face. This happiness might be the start of reborn enthusiasm to bring back the school's sports spirit and in the community.

"First place, 6000m, Lyndon Collins, from Dahmedeh School." Three consecutive gold medals for six categories was not bad at all. That was an excellent achievement for the first tournament of the year.

"WHAAAAT!" Ms. Island said in a surprised voice. In ten years, no teacher had done what Mr. Charles had. Trusting this group of boys to go out of the community was a risk, but it was a breakthrough and an incredible Cinderella story.

"What kind of coach are you? How did you do it?" Mr. Magarwa asked in his text.

Mr. Charles had simply done nothing other than bond and build trust with the boys in the short time he had been in the school. He trusted the boys, and they delivered. The relationship was the best foundation for success. Mr. Charles was so happy that he had found success through first building a relationship with these young people with instant success. It gave a tremendous opportunity for these young people to capitalize and boost their self-confidence that they were good at something. Role models played a significant part in the lives of these growing juveniles. Show them the way, and they will follow. Mr. Charles wished that this success would be the start of another great school year, if not in academics, at least in the field of sports.

On a later date, Mr. Charles realized that there was a Zone Cross Country Running Tournament, and he had not received any information about it. This occurrence was another issue that he intended to find out.

CHAPTER 8

The Wrestling Match with Gaston

"No one will discover that I'm drunk. Everyone is too scared to smell me," Gaston said as he sipped from a "miki" bottle in the washroom. That is what he thought.

Knock! Knock! Knock! Samuel was knocking at Mr. Charles' door.

"Mr. Charles, can I talk to you?" Samuel requested.

Mr. Charles always opened his door to all students. Students loved to visit him in the morning when they got to the school and before they left the building. Mr. Charles made it a habit always of being visible to the children. He knew that somehow children were still longing for his attention and affirmation. Students looked up to him as a father or even as a grandfather. Having spent time in the community for almost twelve years, most of the children were the daughters and sons of his former students.

It was hilarious one time when Mr. Charles was in the hallway of the office.

"Grandpa."

"Grandpa."

"Grandpa!" A little girl was calling him in a small, soft voice. He thought that someone was making fun of him. When he glanced back, he saw Gemma, a second-grade pupil, and his previous student Sherry's daughter.

Mr. Charles smiled; he approached Gemma, knelt to the child's eye level, and hugged her.

"That's right, Gemma; what's the matter?" he inquired.

There was a talent show at that time, and everyone was in their best outfits.

"Can I call my mom? She needs to bring my dress, and she's not even helping. She's always drunk. She said she would bring my outfits after lunch," Gemma said with teary eyes.

Mr. Charles was very compassionate. He understood what the children were experiencing, both at home and in the classroom. Teachers sometimes criticized the way Mr. Charles treated the students. He welcomed them and let them express their feelings. If a child were crying, Mr. Charles would give him or her time to regulate a gesture of respect for their feelings. He always ensured that the child could talk and feel comfortable and composed. Mr. Charles found his happiness by helping young people. He helped students by letting them help themselves and find ways to solve their problems.

"How do you want me to help you, little princess?" Mr. Charles was trying to cheer her up.

After crying, Gemma smiled. "Can I phone her?"

"Do you know her number?" Mr. Charles was trying to find out if children knew the number of their parents. That is one of the skills that a child should learn: answering questions appropriately and finding solutions to their problems.

"Okay, come on in; let's try to call her."

Everything is a teachable moment. A child's engagement and interaction with a nurturing adult are crucial to their learning. Mr. Charles showed her how to dial the number. At that moment, the child learned something essential to her growth.

Working in the office is not that easy. Solving staff issues or getting a daily call from an angry parent can take a toll on one's mental health. Mr. Charles would lead people to find a solution to their problems and make sure they had a win-win result. Angry parents would come out of his office, smiling. Mr. Charles listened to children and adults.

"How come that angry grandma was smiling when she came out of your office, Mr. Charles?" Rhoze wondered.

"Well, what I did was just provide her my open heart and listening ears. It's called empathic listening and undivided attention." Mr. Charles shared his strategy on how to handle difficult parents and guardians.

On Monday, Mr. Charles dealt with Myla, a thirteen-year-old Grade 7 student who struggled to stay in the classroom.

"You're giving in again, Mr. Charles," Mr. Columby, a Grade-7 teacher, said.

"Mr. Columby," Mr. Charles said calmly, "my office provides refuge to every student and staff member in the school. If a child does not feel welcome in the classroom, I will cater to them to stay in school. Our job is to keep them here and accommodate what they need. Remember why we are here. 'Students First' is the motto of the school. It is not what you want. It is how we can accommodate and understand their feelings. We need to establish a strong rapport with the students and their parents to love coming to school. Students will allow you to teach them if you have a secure connection with them and their parents," he explained further.

The staff understood how tough Mr. Charles' job in the office was. He relied more on relationships than on authority, and he would build on the trust of everyone around him to gain respect. That was how he thrived as an administrator.

"Oh, Samuel, what brings you here?" Mr. Charles thought that Samuel was still excited after the cross country running win.

Staff members model positive behaviour, such as knocking at the door or politely asking permission, and that is how students learn ways of having a respectful environment.

"When I went to the boy's washroom, I saw a huge junior high school boy chugging a miki," Samuel reported.

Samuel had gained the confidence to help the school administration to report any unusual student behaviour, especially when it came to alcohol. Samuel recognized the danger of having someone drunk inside the school premises. He also understood the predicament of being addicted to alcohol. He was a victim of it. His siblings transferred from foster home to foster home due to parental addiction to alcohol. Once, his parents were drunk with friends, and they quarreled and caused trouble, which caused them to go to jail. Samuel and his siblings could not go back home unless their parents went to the treatment centre, which they refused to do. They went once; however, as they got back into the community, they indulged again. Even though the village was called a "dry reserve," the people still had ways to acquire liquor.

"Do you know his name, Samuel?" Mr. Charles inquired.

"I think it's Gaston," he responded.

Mr. Charles knew that Gaston was a troubled kid. He liked to drink and could just walk into a liquor store without being asked for identification. He was a bearded and colossal fellow. You would mistake him as a father of three kids.

"Samuel, go and get Garrett from the Grade-2 classroom," Mr. Charles urged.

Garrett was a six-foot-four, giant EA; his mammoth size scared the students. He yelled at kids when he saw them in the hallway. Even though instructed not to shout, Garrett understood that these students needed a disciplinarian—a strict one. It was like the old school ways, to make them learn and be successful someday. Garrett knew that when Mr. Charles sent for him, it was a code-red emergency.

"You and Samuel follow me into the washroom," Mr. Charles instructed them.

"Hello, anyone here?" Mr. Charles inquired.

They then went into the washroom. School staff members were not allowed to go into the students' washroom; that's why he inquired before going inside. Mr. Charles saw a substantial amount of empty miki bottles, but Gaston was not there. They walked down to the junior high school classroom, but they could not find him.

"Where could he be?" Mr. Charles was puzzled.

"I heard a commotion in the gym. Gaston might be there," Samuel answered.

They hurried immediately to the gym. The students were quiet and were watching for an exciting event to unfold to take a video.

"Notify the police!" Mr. Charles asked Henrick.

Gaston started to create trouble. He was intimidating the gym teacher.

"You son of a b***h! F**K y**!" Gaston yelled at the gym teacher.

"You don't know stuff; you're just here for the money!"

Gaston was wobbly and drunk and tried to scare the poor gym teacher. Honestly, most of the gym teachers at the school were cool teachers. Physical education was a favourite subject for most of the children because it was fun. They all played games and, at the same time, learned life lessons such as sportsmanship and respect, which eventually carried over to the classroom.

This kind of incident was the reason why there was a fast turnover of teachers every year. Students were so naughty and were scaring them away. They felt that they were just wasting their energy in this community. People knew that "Dimension" (the former community name) had a horrible name.

When we went to a badminton tournament in the zone, hosted by Sandhill School in River Valley, I remembered the lady at the hotel we checked in.

"Where are you guys from?" the front desk lady inquired while checking the athletes in.

"From Dahmedeh," Mr. Charles responded.

"Where is that?" the lady continued.

"Oh, the former name of the community was 'Dimension.'"

The lady could not believe what she had heard. She seemed shocked and startled. She could not think that the players who behaved respectfully and adequately were from Dimension.

"Oh, Dimension! Scary!" she said.

Mr. Charles just ignored the lady. He had heard so much bad stuff about the community, but that was just stereotyping and racist treatment by people who had never gone to or lived within Dahmedeh.

Just imagine when this gym teacher leaves the community. What news would he share with other professionals looking for a job? He would say not to go there because it's scary.

Before Gaston could grab the gym teacher, Garrett used an armlock and dragged him out of the gym. It was not easy to do that since Gaston was resisting. There was high tension in everyone, but it didn't scare them enough to make them run away; instead, they stayed and watched the clashing of two great warriors—two bull moose were fighting on the ground, and no one wanted to yield.

"You are nothing to me, you son of a b***h!" Gaston mocked Garrett.

A drunk person can cause a lot of harm to a person that doesn't have any martial arts background. Gaston freed himself and knocked Garrett out. Before Mr. Charles could step in, Samuel jumped on Gaston's back.

"I got him, Mr. Charles," Samuel exclaimed.

Samuel grabbed Gaston's neck and made a piggyback move that immobilized him. He tried to shake Samuel off against the wall, but Samuel was like a leech sucking upon Gaston's blood.

Gaston could not escape as Samuel kept squeezing his neck with a powerful half-nelson grip. Mr. Charles helped Samuel control Gaston's elbow by applying his Aikido skills. He grabbed Gaston's wrist and twisted it until he knelt due to excruciating pain.

"My hand, my hand! You f*****g Asian! Gaston shouted in pain.

Samuel was still on Gaston's back, and he didn't get off him until he was lying on the floor unconscious.

Rhoze quickly followed up with 911 and requested police and an ambulance. Gaston was unconscious, and there was a rotten stench around him. He was drunk, and he had passed out. The *miki* must have kicked it very well.

The police arrived at the school, along with an ambulance. The paramedic checked on Gaston. They declared that Gaston was okay and that he was just drunk. He was handcuffed and thrown into jail to regain consciousness.

That night, Mr. Charles guarded Gaston at the police holding jail. He also worked as a part-time guard during the weekend. Because Mr. Charles lived by himself and had nothing to do on Saturdays and Sundays, police guarding was perfect. They had been looking for an extra guard, which was his job before he came to teach at the Dahmedeh Community School.

CHAPTER 9

Melanie and Stephanie's Incident

People expected that there would not be a lot of students in the school on Friday. It was a child tax day, and most parents were taking their children to town for shopping. Students also struggled to get up due to darkness. During wintertime, even at eight o'clock, it is still quite dark. It was too early for the children to wake up, mostly when they slept late due to playing video games. They would be so tired and sleepy at school. Usually, high school boys would just sleep in the classroom, or they skipped class and hid from the teacher.

I caught some students sleeping in their classrooms.

"You're missing a student, Ms. Perez?" Before Ms. Perez answered, Mr. Charles saw Jason lying on the floor, sound asleep. "Mr. Charles, I can explain," said Ms. Perez.

Teachers accommodated children who were sleepy inside the classroom. They would give them time to recuperate to gain the energy to learn. It was quite an effective strategy; however, teachers needed to inform parents about the observed behaviour. The behaviour would become chronic if the school admin never addressed it immediately.

Teachers also sent notes home to remind parents how to monitor their children during night time. Educating parents about the importance of sleep and how it affects their learning is crucial to students' academic progress. The brain cannot function properly if a child has not had enough sleep.

Ms. Stringer, a high school teacher, was an outstanding and seasoned teacher after her experience of teaching in the Calvary Board of Education. She had a comprehensive understanding of the curriculum and how much effort a high school student needed to earn credits. She also told the high school students that if they were not in the classroom, they would be marked absent, which was true. Students, most of the time, had no motivation at all. They thought that coming to school was just for hanging out with friends. Most of the high school students were receiving social assistance money. They should learn how to work hard for their money, like in a "learn and earn" program. However, even if they didn't pass, they knew they still received enough money, even without finishing their education.

In the morning, Melanie and Stephanie were late. Ms. Stringer marked them late, and then, around 10:00 a.m., they went missing. They left the school grounds without asking for permission from their teacher.

Knock! Knock! Knock! Samuel was knocking at Mr. Charles' door.

"I'm glad to see you this Friday, Samuel," Mr. Charles greeted.

It was unusual because Samuel was always late, and it was Friday too. Sometimes he took an early vacation and did not come in on Fridays.

"I felt strange today," Samuel started. "I saw Melanie and Stephanie leave the school grounds. They went to Jonas's house," Samuel said.

Samuel had a right to feel strange because he knew Jonas was a youth offender. He had spent most of his life in juvenile delinquent prison. Fighting people and robbing elders of their pension money was his signature *modus operandi*. I remembered Jonas; he was only in Grade 2 when he stopped coming. He struggled to learn to read and write. He grew up to be a big, tall lad and never went back to school again. He was always in trouble and would target young girls to drink with and then do bad stuff with them. I had overheard that he would touch women when they passed out after drinking.

Mr. Charles paged Ms. Stringer and asked about the two girls.

"We're looking for them, Mr. Charles," Ms. Stringer explained. "They left the school property without asking permission," she added.

Mr. Charles instructed Ms. Stringer to phone the parents of Melanie and Stephanie. It was challenging to contact parents or guardians by phone because they always changed numbers. If the students did not update their phone numbers, it was impossible to get their parents. The school had no liaison officer for a long time due to no funding for the position.

Samuel volunteered to follow up with them. He went to the washroom and closed his eyes. In the winter season, Samuel thought that eagles migrated, but in his vision, they were still screeching in the sky as the wolves hibernated in their den, sending a spiritual signal to him.

As he took a peek outside, two figures emerged in the middle of a wide-open, frosty and frozen field. Samuel ran as fast as he could to check who they were.

"What happened?" he asked.

"She was too heavy," Melanie said, crying.

"She had no boots." She was referring to Stephanie.

The girls had not dressed appropriately for the weather; they were not wearing winter coats or proper winter boots. Stephanie had no socks on and no tuque. Her long hair was not enough to keep her head warm.

"She was too drunk and could not even walk," Melanie sniffled.

Melanie was also tipsy due to a couple of shots. Stephanie was too drunk. She was frostbitten and could not walk, and she was too heavy for Melanie to carry.

"Let me help you," Samuel offered.

He grabbed Stephanie's right hand and put it on top of his shoulder. Melanie was on the other side.

Melanie was shocked. She could not believe what she saw. Samuel, even with his petite size, could carry Stephanie. Melanie and Stephanie were quivering from the cold. The school was at least two more kilometres away.

Mr. Charles put his snow jacket on and checked outside. From afar, he saw three figures. He phoned Wally, the maintenance man, to back him up. Wally was a big and strong guy. He could quickly help when needed. At a closer distance, Mr. Charles saw Samuel.

"Wally, it's Samuel. Let's check if they need help," Mr. Charles said.

Wally helped Samuel carry Stephanie, for she could not move at all. She had passed out and was frostbitten. Samuel gave Stephanie to Wally, and he assisted Melanie, who could barely take another step.

Mr. Charles asked for the help of Ms. Stringer.

"Get Mr. MacDonough, and tell him that Stephanie is unconscious. She is frostbitten, and we need first aid."

Mr. Charles opened the small room with a single size bed inside, and Wally laid her down. She was still unconscious. She had a terrible smell of liquor and was dead drunk.

Ms. Duncan, the high school EA, asked Mr. Lisso for the new blanket that he had in his office. They used it to wrap Stephanie to keep her warm. Rhoze phoned the community first responder. They were on their way as Mr. MacDonough was giving

Stephanie first aid. He was an expert in saving victims of accidents, and this was one of them.

They soaked Stephanie's feet in warm water. The water quickly turned cold. Her feet were like pieces of hard ice, turning the warm water into a cold bath.

After thirty minutes, the community responder arrived. Deanne, Stephanie's auntie, was one of the two responders who came. She phoned Stephanie's mom right away. Most of the time, siblings would keep their sibling's number privately, and it was lucky that Deanne was the auntie. They decided to take Stephanie out of the school and took her to the nurse's station. She needed medical attention; otherwise, she would die.

Melanie felt horrible. "We're bad. Those guys let us drink, and Stephanie just kept chugging those beer bottles. I don't know what's up with her."

In this community, freezing is the most common cause of death. People would drink and pass out, and then, in the morning, they would be found frozen. People just didn't care about their lives or the people they loved. There were lots of people who were grieving because of the loss of loved ones. The community's culture also needed to respect the family by not celebrating some sort when someone passed away. It was like other cultures too.

If it weren't for Samuel, another young person would have died for no reason. People just don't care about these young people. They should not be leaving the school property and just going to drink somewhere. That was not in good character, especially for a young girl that the community would rely upon as its future leader.

The presence of Samuel brought new hope to the community. Luring young girls from the school, and offering them liquor, was not a good practice. Samuel would have liked to teach those people a lesson, but it was outside of the school. He hoped that the proper authorities and agencies would see this social problem that was corrupting young people slowly but surely. Alcohol and drugs were slowly claiming the lives of people in the community. This menace should stop, and the reserve needed to change for the betterment of the younger generations.

CHAPTER 10

The School Break and Entry

The teachers' compound was just outside the school fence. From the window of the unit, one could see the full view of the school building. It is adjacent and very convenient for teachers because they can walk to work every day. It was also a habit for Mr. Charles to check out his kitchen window and glance at the school before going to bed. Sometimes young people roamed the schoolyard late at night because that was the only building they could hang around. It was not too bad if these young people stayed around in the schoolyard if they took care of the school and caused no harm. But they would either vandalize the building by writing graffiti on the wall or even attempt to break the windows and make a forced entry.

I recalled that even though the school had an alarm, it was not safe from break and entries. The gang would usually target the school for break-ins, especially during spring, summer, and fall, when people are more active. Juvenile delinquency was rampant in the community as they stay out late at night, even when there is an active curfew. I noticed that young people are not scared of the police. They view breaking the law as fun and exciting. I think it is a natural tendency for teenagers, especially when they live in a community without offering them many activities. Since I came to the community, I have always opened the gym for volleyball, floor hockey, basketball, and badminton nights. People like to play when they are in the mood for playing. Sometimes the attendance is very sporadic. Sometimes I only played with my son.

Channo would always play with us. After he finished playing basketball, he would ask permission to go to the weight room to finish his workout.

"It's fun to play basketball, Mr. Charles. Thank you for doing the open gym night. It's good for us young people. I used to break in this school, and I biked in this gym," he confessed.

"Why did you do that?" I inquired.

"We couldn't sleep during the night time, and there's nothing to do in this community. It's too boring. We did it for fun," he casually said. "We just waited for the alarm to go off and waited for the cops to show up. Then we would go fast on our bikes and make them chase us. It was so much fun. They could never catch us. We were good at hiding."

One cold evening, during the first heavy snowfall, no one anticipated that the gang would attack the school. The alarm sounded, and there was no doubt that someone had forced entry. Ms. Island, the vice-principal, quickly went to her truck and drove to the school, hoping that the intruders were still inside the building. When the alarm sounded like that, the alarm company would call my number and dispatch police officers. She was right. Four young people hurried out of the building and ran in separate directions. Two boys ran towards the arena, and the other two ran towards Trailer Court. They were all laughing.

"HOOOOOOOOOO, that's so fun!" was all you could hear, breaking the silence of the cold night.

The school's back alley was relatively narrow, but it was wide enough for an excellent driver to squeeze a long Ford F150 through, untouched. Ms. Island damaged her truck. She miscalculated the right turn during that night. The steel fence protecting the electrical box scratched the side of her vehicle. She was concentrating more on chasing the intruders than focusing on her driving. She spent at least two-thousand-five-hundred dollars for that damage as she did not even claim it on her insurance. She did not want to increase her premium. I was wondering why she needed to do that. She was not a cop either to implement a law. I understood her dedication and commitment to protecting the school, but how could she get these young boys? Was she going to handcuff them? No way. These boys would not listen. She did not have to catch these boys. She would just have to know who the intruders were, and then the cops would do the arresting tomorrow.

The police officers arrived at the scene. They went around the school building and checked how the intruders had got into the building. There was shattered glass at the front of the door, on the junior high side. It showed that the intruders used rocks to break the windows. Corporal Sutherland requested Wally to check on the camera.

"Can you burn a CD for this incident, Wally, if you find something?" asked the corporal.

Wally checked on the camera. It showed five boys in hoodies had grabbed rocks, smashed the junior high school computer laboratory window, and used it as their entry point. The boys imitated what they had seen in a movie. As they walked down the hallway, they pretended that they were doing a raid. They simulated what they had watched. They used their hands to pretend that they had a gun. The other boy used a crowbar as his long gun. They forcefully used a crowbar to get into the office. After several strikes, they managed to open the locked door. They opened all the drawers and filing cabinets, and they scattered a lot of things on the floor. They left the filing cabinets open, and it was evident that they were searching for something. Loose change was everywhere on the floor.

On their way out, they also pulled out the fire extinguishers and squirted all the white stuff on the floor. They even tried to target the camera. They knew that no one could recognize them because they were wearing their masks. As they had expected, Wally could not remember the boys. He could just assume, but he could not identify them. The police officers tried to look for a lead, but people wouldn't talk. It would just be a witch hunt because people would protect their kind. Wally could only replace the broken windows and forget everything as if nothing had happened.

Thelma, the fundraising committee coordinator, was looking for the money that the students had raised as it was missing. Those boys broke into the school because of that money. The camera could not prove anything due to the intruders wearing masks. They were aware that the school had an alarm and cameras, but they did not care, and it didn't stop them from getting the cash they wanted. There was not much money circulating in the community and not many jobs around, so young people chose to look for easy money.

"Monkey see, monkey do," was the American adage during the 1920s. Little children will copy what the adults are showing them. One weekend, Wally called and invited me inside the server room, where the cameras were available to review. He showed me two boys, Phantom and Reymar, smashing the window with big rocks. I assured Wally that I would call their parents to explain the record.

I spoke with Phantom about the incident of the broken window last Saturday. He denied it and pointed out Reymar as being the only one smashing the window with the rocks.

"I told him not to do it, but he didn't listen," Phantom explained.

He was right; the camera only showed Reymar doing the smashing while Phantom was watching. I called Jonnalyn, the mother of Reymar, to show her what her son had been doing during the weekend. I also took Reymar to the server room to see what he was doing last Saturday.

"Who's this Reymar?" I inquired after showing him the recorded footage.

"That's not me," Reymar denied.

"What!" the mom yelled. "What a liar. It's you! Can't you recognize yourself?" the mom insisted.

Even though he got caught, Reymar would never admit that he was the one smashing the window. He was blaming Phantom. Just imagine when Reymar grows up a little bit more. You can see a self-fulfilling prophecy starting to emerge. One can easily predict that this boy will grow up like the others. There is no consideration or respect for parents and the building. Another member of young offenders was starting to develop.

To avoid this incident from happening, the Operation and Maintenance Department hired a night guard. The break-ins stopped for a little while. They knew that there was a guard inside the school, so they could not get in. They would get caught. Everything should have gone smoothly, but one night there was a break-in. Ms. Island found out that the guard kept submitting a timesheet but was not on duty. He clocked in, leave and come back to clock out. They let the guard go. They replaced with someone, but it was no different. The work ethics needs to improve to serve the community better. With or without a guard, the school is still there. Even if they proved who broke windows, they could not punish the offender. There was no accountability. They tried to send an invoice to parents or guardians, and even the probation officer got involved after a court hearing; still, the behaviour never improved.

The frequent break and entries became less and less, and then they stopped, maybe because these young people had grown up or because they were locked up in jail for so many years. Hopefully, other young people had proper direction and guidance from parents and guardians. Grandparents also have a crucial role in making these young people behave and improve themselves to become productive community members.

An incident such as break and entry is like an upheaval of a volcano. After being dormant for a hundred years, expect the unexpected. A recent break and entry incident occurred in the fall. But the latest event was a little more brutal. The five young people got caught, with bruises, and all were smacked to the ground when the police officers arrived at the school after an anonymous phone call. When Wally checked on the camera, six young people were close to the door, on the junior high side. There were five people on one side of the door, facing another person on the other side of the door. It showed an individual wearing a wolf mask, trying to stop the group from entering the building.

"If I were you, I would not do that," the masked lad warned the group, who were about to smash the glass.

"How about you being the one to get smashed?" the leader said.

"Get out of our way if you don't want to get hurt," the group leader demanded.

"Why would I do that?" the masked boy answered.

"Our grandpa would like us to get something from inside that building. You can't stop us!"

"Oh, I see!" the masked boy replied. "And who is your grandpa?"

"You don't have to know. My grandpa has the medicine, and you will pay for it if you resist," the leader warned.

The action began. The group of boys attacked the masked boy. To their surprise, the masked boy moved very quickly. He could leap so high, like a wolf attacking its prey. He jumped over his attackers and ran around the school.

"Chase him!" shouted the leader. They forgot about their purpose for getting inside the building. The masked boy was faster than any of them. After leaving them behind, he jumped off the ledge of the roof and just watched them. He waited until the boys separated ways, and then he began to surprise them one by one.

The boy with the mask quietly followed a boy who was approaching the shop door. He did not waste time; he smacked him to the ground. The lad could not retaliate for the surprise attack. The boy with the mask tied him up and pulled him aside.

"Did you see him? Did you see him?" Their voices were so loud.

"I could not find him; I think he was scared," one responded.

Another boy was walking towards the park. The masked boy slowly went ahead and then showed himself to him.

"I saw him! I saw him!" the boy shouted.

The masked boy ran back to the school and waited by the door for whoever arrived first. He tripped the first boy, and he never gave him a chance to get up. He grabbed the boy's hands behind his back, tied him up quickly, and carried him away. He hid him at the end of the shed at the front of the school. He promptly went back around the school by the elementary side. The other boys were confused.

"Show yourself. We'll see how tough you are," the group challenged the masked boy.

"I'm here!" the masked boy said.

He intentionally waited at the front door. The light was brighter, and it would give him more visuals to defend himself. This time, he wanted to test his skills. He learned some self-defense moves from Mr. Charles. Watching self-defense videos on YouTube is not enough to learn the skills, so he had asked Mr. Charles to show and share with him some steps.

Young people were good at throwing haymaker punches. They would not have any chance of winning if they didn't have martial arts training. The masked boy seemed to have one, and he showed them well by sweeping their feet. He smacked their faces and gave them quick kicks and punches, which they never saw coming. They were incapable of subduing the smart, skinny masked lad. They were all on the ground, tied up, and could not move.

"Who is that s****d b***h?" they said.

"You will pay. We're going to hunt you! My grandpa will get revenge," they grumbled.

There were no more breaks and entries from then on, for there was an anonymous school guardian.

The end of the school year went great. There were lots of students at the end-of-year Celebration of Success. The children received all their awards. The school recognized all the children's efforts and ensured that every child mattered. Everyone worked as hard as everyone else.

"Before we end our celebration, for the first time, there is a student who would like to share his thoughts with everyone. Children and everyone, let's welcome Samuel Yaluk." Mr. Charles proudly introduced Samuel.

"Samuel! Samuel! Samuel!" The children were chanting his name.

The End

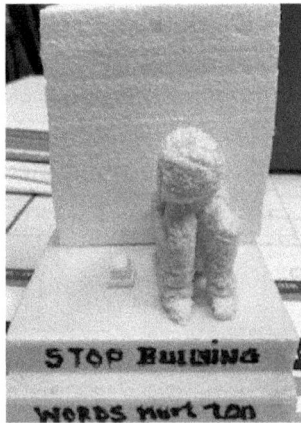

Styrofoam sculpture by Walter Beaulieu

ABOUT THE AUTHOR

Carlito N. Somera has been an educator for almost 30 years. *Facing Your Fears* is his first published book of fiction, inspired by authentic life experiences during his career. He holds a Bachelor of Secondary Education (English) degree from Mt. Carmel College, Baler, Aurora, his province. He finished his Master of Arts in English Language Teaching Academic Requirements at the Philippine Normal University. He holds his Master's of Arts in Education (Language Education) from the University of the Philippines, Diliman, and enrolled in some courses at the University of Alberta Open University. Carlito grew up in the Philippines, and in 2004 moved to Canada, lived in Edmonton for three years, and worked as a Teacher Assistant in Edmonton Public School. In 2007, he started teaching at the Dene Tha' Community School in Chateh, Alberta, a community he considers home. Carlito has experienced to persevere the toughness of life, and after six years, he worked as Vice-Principal of the school and the current principal. He believes that to thrive in a particular place, you need to know the people and establish a healthy relationship. They are the strongest allies you can have by your side to teach their children.

www.ingramcontent.com/pod-product-compliance
Lightning Source LLC
Chambersburg PA
CBHW070500090426
42735CB00012B/2631